ONE NATION UNDER A GROOVE

Motown and American Culture

GERALD EARLY

Revised and Expanded Edition

One

Nation

Under a

Groove

Motown and American Culture

Gerald Early

University of Michigan Press
Ann Arbor

OCM 53900284

To Mr. Lloyd Richard King,
my teacher,
who always believed in me.
Would that I were always worthy
of that great faith.

Copyright © 1995, 2004 by Gerald Early
Published by the University of Michigan Press 2004
First published by the Ecco Press 1995
All rights reserved
Published in the United States of America by
The University of Michigan Press
Manufactured in the United States of America
⊚ Printed on acid-free paper

2007   2006   2005   2004   4   3   2   1

A CIP catalog record for this book is available from the British Library.

Grateful acknowledgment is made to the following authors, publishers,
and journals for permission to reprint previously published materials:

Billboard Magazine for "Just the Music" by David Nathan, *Billboard*
Magazine, October 23, 1993; "Stevie Wonder: 35th Anniversary Salute
Interview" by David Nathan, *Billboard Magazine,* May 13, 1995; and
"Gordy Speaks: The Billboard Interview" by Adam White, *Billboard*
Magazine. © copyright 1993, 1995 by VNU BUSINESS MEDIA, INC.
Used with permission from *Billboard®.*

The article "What's Really Going On With Marvin Gaye?" by Patrick
William Salvo was originally published in *Sepia* 27, no. 4 (April 1978):
14–22.

Every effort has been made to trace the ownership of all copyrighted material
in this book and to obtain permission for its use.

ISBN 0-472-08956-0

Contents

Introduction

In recent years, as I became more and more identified as someone with expertise in popular culture or with an intellectual predisposition toward popular culture and its study, I grew more wary of both the subject and my association with it. I could think of nothing I wanted less than such an identification; not, as it were, that this disinclination was the outgrowth of any sort of dislike of the subject or the squeamishness connected with the act of being exposed at "slumming," after all. That some of my colleagues might feel the subject to be something of an indulgence or a squandering of time and talent that can rightly be traced to Rousseau having come into the world is not, frankly, a major worry, as I never wholly believed myself to be a guardian of the culture, although I am by no means bashful about enjoying the perks and privileges, the overall sense of cultivation, of being part of an elite. My interest in popular culture does not generate from so vainglorious and heroic a source as the need to identify with the working classes or the masses, nor as an expression of contempt against the status conferred upon high culture. I am not so childishly egalitarian as that, or as the working-class boys with whom I grew up used to put it when fiercely competing on the playground, "If you want my respect, you gotta earn it." Besides, to paraphrase an old saw, I've been working class and I've been middle class and middle class is better, taken all around, even if to earn someone's respect these days all I have to do primarily is be willing to buy it.

Rather, I have felt as if such an identification with popular culture were not, to use a phrase, "truth in advertising." My interest in popular culture is narrow, almost to the point of being a small series of points, perhaps of light, but surely not as benighted as some might think: namely, boxing, baseball, boys' literature at the turn of the century, and jazz. This list seems to take modesty to a new depth of complete unassumingness. (And I might add that I have so assiduously avoided the possible taint of "expertise" that I have never considered teaching any of these subjects as courses; that would strike me as being both bizarre and unintelligible.) I never wanted to be one of those intellectuals who hung around kitsch because it was hip, easy to write about, and, with a cynical mixture of appreciation and gratitude, easy to make a reputation with because one was destined, in writing about it, always to sound smarter than the subject at hand. With varying degrees of interest I read theories about popular culture (of which there is no small number) and the political interpretations these theories suggest. I have never been interested in constructing any of my own, although some might suppose this book makes gestures in that direction. I will explain to them that the book is a "meditation on," not a "theory about."

Motown, the subject of this small book, was never a passion of mine. I appreciate the music, am deeply fond of much of it, but I was not driven to write about it simply from a nostalgic urge (the most sentimental and often misguided corruption of both the past and the present) to talk about a popular music with which I grew up. A hazard lurked, as real as the romanticization of personal memory, behind the allure of writing about something so closely associated with growing up, of being drawn to it simply because one is, naturally, drawn with pain and pleasure to one's childhood and adolescence. Something else, larger and more dispassionately demanding, was what had to be pursued here. There were other matters I wished to tackle in looking at Motown, specifically about African-American life and culture in the 1950s, 1960s, and 1970s, not fully explored but tentatively mapped out for fuller exploration in some future book or two. Indeed, I see this brief effort as something like a prelude and fugue to some deeper studies that—imagining them as something like grand symphonies—would be attractive to fewer readers, if only because, wishing to aspire to greater invention, they run a greater risk of being such utter failures.

Leon Wieseltier of the *New Republic* approached me a few years ago to write an article on Motown. I would never have thought of it myself and indeed had never thought about it until the very moment of being challenged by Mr. Wieseltier's offer. Why he approached me I do not know, unless he too saw me as something like a pop culture guy or perhaps a music guy since I had written some pieces about jazz or perhaps a polemics guy since I am black. (In the case of pop culture, I certainly do not put myself in the class of, say, Nelson George, or in the case of jazz writing, in the class of Stanley Crouch, or in the case of polemics, in the class of, say, Ralph Wiley or Thomas Sowell or bell hooks. I am compelled by modesty and sheer common sense to make that small confession so that, as sometimes happens in this society, I am not confused with any other black man or woman who writes for a living; there being, to use Moses' phrase, undeniably, "a confusion of tongues" among African-Americans.) What was ultimately published in the pages in that magazine was perhaps 60 to 70 percent of the original manuscript, although as Mr. Wieseltier reassured me through his competent editing, the final published version, basically maintaining the integrity of the original, was among the longer pieces that the *New Republic* ever published.

This book is, in fact, much closer to what I had in mind when I finished the piece for Mr. Wieseltier, a miniepic meditation on two ideas. The first is that Motown was important because it helped to crystallize the formation, not of a black audience (that had existed before), but of a black public and a black public taste that was taken seriously as an expression of a general aesthetic among a broad class of Americans. The creation of a black public—a body of black folk who have no connection with each other or commitment to each other except the idea that they are consumers whose consumption is given meaning because of their race—is, I think, a very different abstraction from the idea of a black community.

Second, Motown, an extraordinary success in the realm of mass culture or popular culture, actually helped to bring into clear definition the taste and urges of a middle-brow black audience whose existence helped to create such middle-brow black conceptions as Afrocentrism, the name African-American, and the mythology of the black community. Jazz had been, until the 1950s, a low-brow music of Broadway tunes and blues-based improvisations that aspired to be middle-brow. It turned into a high-brow expression when it became self-consciously obsessed by all varieties of *composition* and completely left the realm of popular dance, leaving a void in African-American culture that was filled nicely by Motown.

In short, it is my hope that I might have more to say about Motown than that it was a successful black record company, a successful black business, or that, alas, white folk liked the music. This last point, in some measure, seems to me to be especially trivial as whites were always admirers of black music and have always, for some reason, felt compelled to make a histrionic point of it. That Motown was the soundtrack for *The Big Chill* seems less important than the fact that it was the soundtrack for *Nothing But a Man*, a film that may be more important for all our children in the long run. But then again, I am much of the mind that Alan Freed's cheap, awful rock-and-roll "documentaries" are of greater significance in talking about miscegenation than, say, *Blackboard Jungle*, our first rock-and-roll film, as it is commonly called. It is my hope that most of this or, at least, some of it, will be made a bit clearer here than it may have been in the piece as it was printed in the *New Republic*.

I want to thank my wife, Ida, and our daughters, Linnet and Rosalind, for having to put up with so many hours of hearing me talk about Motown and for so many hours of listening to Motown records. This last, though, was not so bad as all that and everyone always wound up singing and dancing the night away.

Finally, I would like to thank Theo Broughton, a fine woman, without whose generous assistance I would not have been able to complete the original *New Republic* article or this book.

Straight Ahead   St. Louis, Missouri
Gerald Early   August 8, 1994

                                            Revised
                                            January 18, 2003

Addendum to Introduction

I have made some corrections to the text of this edition of *One Nation Under a Groove,* mostly correcting grammar, stylistic infelicities, or factual misstatements. I have added endnotes to elaborate upon some points made in the text. I have also added a bibliography because writing about Motown has exploded since the original publication of *One Nation Under a Groove* and I thought readers might wish to know about other books, including those I originally consulted. In case you are wondering if I would have radically changed anything in the text as a result of what later books have said about Motown, the answer is no. I am surprised, in fact, by how well my assertions and analysis have held up. Finally, I have added a set of appendixes that include edited reprints of interviews with several Motown stars. I thought the reader might find this useful.

Gerald Early
St. Louis, Missouri
Martin Luther King, Jr., Day, 2003

Family

Happiness

One generation passeth away . . .

How can, Oh, how can those enemies but say that we and
our children are not of the HUMAN FAMILY . . .

—David Walker's *Appeal to the Colored Citizens
of the World*

My dream was to become Frank Sinatra. I loved his
phrasing, especially when he was very young and pure. He
grew into a fabulous jazz singer and I used to fantasize
about having a lifestyle like his—carrying on in
Hollywood and becoming a movie star. Every woman in
America wanted to go to bed with Frank Sinatra. He was
the king I longed to be. My greatest dream was to satisfy
as many women as Sinatra. He was the heavyweight
champ, the absolute.
Now this is going to surprise you, but I also dug Dean
Martin and especially Perry Como. They weren't monster
singers, but I liked their relaxed presentation. Perry had a
great attitude. When I finally got some money together
over at Motown in the sixties, I used to sport Perry
Como's sweaters. I always felt like my personality and
Perry's had a lot in common.

—Marvin Gaye, from David Ritz's *Divided Soul: The Life of
Marvin Gaye*

This organization is built on love.
—Berry Gordy, Jr. about Motown, *Newsweek*, March 22, 1965

The African-American and the Italian

It is one of the peculiar and penetrating gestures of "crossover" in American culture that in the 1960s, Marvin Gaye could fantasize about being an Italian pop ballad singer, making four ballads-and-standards albums for Motown between 1961 and 1965, while the Italian singers of the Rascals could fantasize about being black soul singers with such songs for Atlantic as "Good Lovin'" (1966) and "Groovin'" (1967), which topped the R and B charts. This fantasy-swapping-cum-mutual-admiration seems an old business with blacks and Italians in music: The legendary guitarist Eddie Lang was born Salvatore Massaro and often recorded under the name of Blind Willie Dunn, as if he were a black country musician. On the other hand, bass saxophonist Adrian Rollini had no bigger admirers than Coleman Hawkins and Harry Carney, and there was the great black opera star of the 19th century, Thomas Bowers, who was called "The Colored Mario" because he sounded so much like Italian tenor Giovanni Mario.

Considering the blatant sexual nature of most popular American dance music ("We're selling sex," Paul Williams reminded his fellow Temptations as they donned their form-fitting trousers), both Gaye and The Rascals betrayed a kind of sexual envy of the other's ethnic identity. A strange affair for two ethnic groups that never liked one another very well. For example, the Detroit race riot of 1942, fought, in part, over the issue of housing and leisure space, was largely, though not exclusively, a conflict between blacks and Italians. No matter how that may have turned out, certainly blacks thought when middleweight champion Sugar Ray Robinson flattened Rocky Graziano in three rounds in Chicago in 1952 that some score between the two groups had just been evened. They remembered, for example, when Dodger outfielder Carl Furillo and third baseman Cookie Lavagetto signed a petition in 1947, along with some die-hard southerners, saying that they would never play on the same team as Jackie Robinson. More recently, the first three of Sylvester Stallone's *Rocky* movies have exploited the conflict between blacks and Italians to great box-office advantage.[1]

In the beginning of the fifties and well into the middle years of that decade, Italian male pop-crooners and melodramatic operatic tenors ruled popular music: Julius La Rosa, Al Martino, Dean Martin, Tony Bennett, Vic Damone, Mario Lanza, Frankie Laine, Jerry Vale, and Perry Como. The reigning prince was, of course, Frank Sinatra. The 1950s witnessed two major shifts in popular music: first, a movement away from the Tin Pan Alley–type popular songs of the Berlin-Gershwin-Arlen ilk to a music that was more obviously and overtly influenced by, and openly mimicked, black Rhythm and Blues; second, a shift away from middle-aged or mature-sounding Italian male singers as kings of the popular roost toward white Southerners, adolescent Jewish songwriters, and blacks as the trendsetters in popular music, a major ethnic shift that had a profound impact on the culture at large.

By the very early 1960s there were still several Italian male singers who, as teen idols, figured prominently in the "new music" called Rock and Roll: Bobby Rydell and Frankie Avalon (both discovered by Paul Whiteman, the WASP bandleader-turned-personality disc jockey, and purveyor of symphonic jazz in the 1920s, who was known in his heyday as "The King of Jazz"), Bobby Darin, Fabian, Frankie Valli of the Four Seasons, Joey Dinicola of Joey Dee and the Starliters, and Dion DiMucci of Dion and the Belmonts. Despite their success, these acts were not the major forces in pop music that the Italian singers in the 1950s had been. Herein lies our tale: The two most successful of the Italian Rock and Roll brigade of the early sixties, Frankie Valli and the Four Seasons on the one hand and Bobby Darin on the other, are the Alpha and Omega representations of the shift in popular music. The Four Seasons were originally signed by and recorded their first three million–selling hits for Vee Jay Records, a Chicago-based, largely (though by no means exclusively) Rhythm and Blues company, owned by blacks. Bobby Darin made his last album in 1972 for Motown Records, the most successful independent record company and the most successful black-owned business in American history. What follows is one story—of Frank Sinatra and the Great Displacement in American pop-culture mythology.

Because the election of John Kennedy, for whom Frank Sinatra campaigned ardently, was touted as a new beginning, the force with which the 1960 Frank Sinatra film *Ocean's 11* announced, ironically, the end of an era, is all the more striking, surrounded as that film is by a kind of modernistic despair. The fifties had been a strange decade for Sinatra—the years of his most profound career defeats and his most startling career triumphs. Among the negatives were the messy divorce from his first wife, Nancy; the much-publicized love affair with Ava Gardner, who became his second wife; the economic downfall of the big-band era after World War II—the era that had made Sinatra a "teen" or bobbysoxer star and shaped his aesthetic vision; the subsequent downturn in Sinatra's record sales, which resulted in his being dropped by the most prestigious of all American record companies, Columbia, in 1952; and the box-office failure of the 1952 film *Meet Danny Wilson* (actually, one of his more peculiar formulaic films from the early period), after all of which Sinatra seemed irretrievably on the skids. How the Academy Award–winning role of

Maggio in the 1953 film *From Here to Eternity* and the 1953 contract with Capitol, the only record company at the time that had even a remote interest in Sinatra, revived his career is now well known. Sinatra went on to become a major box-office attraction in the 1950s, and his Capitol records are now considered perhaps his best work; they certainly reestablished him as king of the pop hill. He sold more records in the 1950s than any other artist, finally managing to replace, in fact and as icon, Bing Crosby, as American's greatest pop singer (although, to be sure, Crosby still sold well). Sinatra became, without question, at this time, the most magnetic Italian presence in American popular culture, eclipsing even the Yankee Clipper, Joe DiMaggio, despite DiMaggio's brief marriage to Marilyn Monroe—one of the stranger celebrity unions—and his incredible success at being able to remain nothing more (or less) than Joe DiMaggio from the day he retired on December 11, 1951.

After the death in 1957 of Humphrey Bogart, a man he greatly admired, Sinatra became the head of the Rat Pack, also called the Clan, an influential nonconformist group of the Hollywood hip that included Dean Martin, Sammy Davis, Jr., Judy Garland, Peter Lawford, Lauren Bacall, Debbie Reynolds, Shirley MacLaine, Joey Bishop, Billy Wilder, and Sammy Cahn and Jimmy Van Heusen (virtually Sinatra's personal songwriters, who penned several Academy Award–winning or nominated hits for his films of the 1950s, including "The Tender Trap," "All the Way," "High Hopes," and "The Second Time Around"). It was the famous Hollywood family of playboys and playgirls, of ethnic outcasts—Italians (Sinatra, Martin), Jews (Cahn, Bishop), blacks (Davis, who was also a Jew)—whose inclusive exclusivity (No Squares, Finks, Mice, or Losers Need Apply!) was an ironic commentary on the racial bigotry or exclusive inclusivity of the Ku Klux Klan, a hate group revived in the heat of the civil rights movement of the 1950s whose victims were largely blacks, Jews, and Italians, and other Catholics. (As Ralph Abernathy commented during the 1965 Selma march, "The only ones they hate more than Negroes down here are Roman Catholics. . . .")

Sinatra had, in fact, established a white, liberal onscreen persona in the 1958 Delmer Daves World War II film *Kings Go Forth,* where he played a working-class sergeant in France who falls in love with Natalie Wood, who, he learns, is biracial, the daughter of a white mother and black father. The Sinatra character, at first, experiences a moment of prejudice but so loves Wood that he overcomes it. She does not feel a sexual attraction toward him. Tony Curtis—ironically, since he is Jewish—plays a rich WASP soldier, a jazz player and charmer, who has a momentary dalliance with Wood but devastates her when he abandons her, unable and, more important, unwilling, to overcome his racism. The film is particularly frank and undoubtedly shocking for its day in having Wood's mother talk about her passionate love for a black man, her late husband, and how they were unable to live in the United States with their child. (The film suggests, among other things, that miscegenation is impossible to acknowledge in America which, one supposes, many black American expatriates already knew.) *Kings Go Forth* generally was in keeping with the kind of problem-of-race film that was being made at the time. Indeed, Wood's tragic mulatto character was a throwback to something like the first *Imitation of Life* film[2] in 1934, except that it was more convincing to hear the late Freddie Washington, a light-skinned Negro, in the adaptation of Fannie Hurst novel, say she was ashamed of being black than it was to hear Wood, a white, say in *Kings Go Forth* that she was proud of being a Negro!

In part, Sinatra's liberalism may be a direct outgrowth of his association with swing music, specifically, and jazz, generally, music that tended to emphasize the democratic impulses of the culture within a strict system of meritocracy. It might be accurately said that the swing-music era was racist, with white bands getting most of the publicity and money. (It must be noted here that Sinatra has made records with the two major black jazz bands of American popular-music history, Count Basie and Duke Ellington, where both black band leaders were given equal billing with him.) Nonetheless, several black swing bands did reasonably well during the 1930s and 1940s, and, more important, popular music in America became openly integrated both on record and in public performance during this time. Jazz, in its relentless professionalism, encouraged, even created, a pluralistic elite, as Lewis A. Erenberg notes: ". . . swing was profoundly cosmopolitan, including blacks, Jews, Italians, Poles, Irish, and Protestant leaders, players, and singers." In some sense, the Rat Pack, the Clan, resembled the pluralistic impulse of the swing music that Sinatra has never ceased to love.

Despite his enormous success and power in the fifties, Sinatra was witnessing, in the arena of popular culture where hipness was being defined anew, the very elements of his own demise as a force due to the sheer inescapable fact that he was too old to be hip any longer. The very same inchoate structure of the youth culture that made him a pop success in the 1940s—mostly, though not entirely, made up of adolescent white girls (Shirley Temple's mediocre 1942 film, *Miss Annie Rooney,* in which she played a working-class teenager in love with big bands, revealed that teenaged girls were already a force as a popular music audience long before Rock and Roll appeared)—were to declare him irrelevant by 1960. As *Life* magazine wrote in a 1958 article on the Clan, Sinatra was more than the "reigning social monarch," "the prophet" of a new social order in Hollywood. He was the "angry middle-aged man," and, in the light of the rise of Rhythm and Blues and Rock and Roll, he became the first and most public of Americans of this age to have a temper tantrum about becoming old when so much of his appeal was based on a youth and hipness that had passed him by.

Ocean's 11, a misogynistic hallucination featuring the extended Rat Pack or Clan—Sinatra, Davis, Martin, Lawford, Bishop, Henry Silva, and Richard Conte, as well as women fellow travelers, Angie Dickinson and MacLaine—tells the tale of eleven ex-World War II paratroopers who band together to rob five Las Vegas casinos with a bit of ingenuity and derring-do. The film is actually a paean of old-style masculine hip by the family to itself, but it seems to lack both energy and sincerity. Sinatra and his friends, in a film that seems like an infantile frat-house joke, are engaged in a sort of last gasp, the final ideological assault of old-fashioned swing—an oxymoronic virtue of "cool" indulgence—against the hedonistic decadence and nihilism of the era of Rock and Roll. These slightly overaged playboys, exhibiting all the symptoms of a midlife crisis, decide to turn back the clock and become adventurers again as they had been in the army.[3] The fact that Sinatra himself and most of the Clan's major players, such as Martin and Lawford, never served in the army, and the fact that it would have been impossible for Sammy Davis—who did actually serve in the armed forces—to have been in the same outfit with the others during World War II, inasmuch as the army was segregated, are curious and telling fantasies and anachronisms.

When the men gather around a pool table—that sign of a tough, working-class boyhood and of the hip, masculine adult as a hustling "adept"—to discuss their plans for robbing Las Vegas, a strange note of confession is sounded when Dean Martin's character criticizes the whole enterprise:

> I like to swing like the rest of you guys but you haven't got a plan here, you've got a pipeload. This ain't a combat team, it's an alumni meeting.

He further elaborates when Sinatra's character, Danny Ocean, asks him what is wrong with the plan:

> For one thing . . . fifteen years. Any of you liars want to claim you're half the man you were in '45? Can you run as fast? Can you think as fast? Can you mix it up as good as you used to? Well, I sure can't. And Danny, if you want to try to catch lightning in a bottle, you go ahead. But don't try to catch yesterday. Old times are only good when you've had 'em.

Martin's words are not heeded by the others and he himself finally falls in line and the story proceeds. It is the film's sincerest moment; the rest, after it is decided to proceed with this perverse rumination, is tripe in the name of revolt against the new order.

Oddly, in the screenplay about robbing casinos, the Pack gives the impression of biting the hand that feeds them, as they were all well-known Vegas lounge acts. But once again, there is the air of this being something of an inside joke. It is well to remember that after World War II, with Vegas the gambling capital of America and the coming in 1955 of Disneyland, the most famous theme park in history, capital investment was concentrated in the West, creating, in essence, playgrounds for adults and children, hedonistic spaces that juxtaposed the fantasy of wholesome, bourgeois fun for the family (American pietism) with the fantasy of getting rich without effort and a sybarite lifestyle (American sin). All of this simultaneously was, if not a new order itself, then perhaps a determined reactionism to uphold the status quo, which in America constantly needs to be rescued from the taint of modernity—even as, in the case of Las Vegas and Disneyland, they genuflect, in their invention, to this extravagantly abundant modernity—as an act of homage to the glories of the past. It might be said that the film, in its confusion, was an attack against a certain manifestation of mass culture by people who had been made possible by it.

The shadow that looms over *Ocean's 11,* that provoked Martin's moment of honesty, that very unexpectedly aged the nonconformist congeries of white hipsters of the 1950s—from Mailer to Sinatra, from the Beat to the Pack—into a kind of outraged and bewildered, threatened and uneasy establishment, was Rock and Roll, which seemed to conjure forth even more miscegenation, unbridled and puerile, unsettling and more egalitarian, than the hipness of jazz, now stodgy and high-hat, could ever have envisioned.

 Basically, rock 'n' roll—which has little musical
eloquence—is a singer's highly personal way of shouting

or moaning lyrics ("The Big Sound"), mostly to a slow,
heavily accentuated four-four time ("The Big Beat"),
accompanied by guitar or hoarse-honked tenor
saxophone. It is eight years old but only in the past two or
three years has it proven that it is more than a flash in the
piano.

—"Rock 'N' Roll Rolls On 'N' On," *Life Magazine,*
December 22, 1958

In November 1957, a piece by Sinatra—entitled "The
Diplomacy of Music"—appeared in a magazine called
Western World. In it he juxtaposed the cool world of jazz
and the hip heat of Rock and Roll by discussing the State
Department-sponsored trips of jazzmen like trumpeters
Louis Armstrong, the "Uncle Tom-ish" old guard
Dixielander, and Dizzy Gillespie, the racially conscious
be-bopper, to the Middle East and Europe. As late as
1949, an editorial in *Ebony* magazine had stated: "The
long war between boppist and anti-boppist factions was
almost political in its defenses. Boppists likened themselves to revolutionary leftists, their opponents as
money-grabbing capitalists. Now, as the battle draws to
a close, boppists find themselves in a musical equivalent
of a political underground." That Armstrong and
Gillespie should be yoked together when they represented such different approaches to the art of improvisa-
tional music—indeed, approaches, no matter how rooted
in the blues or the pop song "standard," that were, to
some, political counterstatements to one another—is a
striking example of how acceptable and even respectable

jazz had become, despite the fact that Charlie Parker's highly publicized death had occurred just two years earlier and the drug-related deaths of Lester Young and Billie Holiday were to occur two years later. (Obviously, to send Armstrong and Gillespie abroad was to show the rest of the "colored world"—an all-too-real political specification in the anti–European-colonialism world of 1950s Asia and Africa—that white America could revere two colored men and could, indeed, send them forth as practitioners of a respected, indigenous art form.)

In two of the most famous youth films of the 1950s, *Blackboard Jungle* and *Jailhouse Rock,* jazz was in fact portrayed as being virtually the property of "intellectuals," "teachers," "authority figures," almost a reactionary art form of egregious pretension. (It is only in a film like Alan Freed's *Mister Rock and Roll* that one sees the radical connection between jazz, Rhythm and Blues, and Rock and Roll in the figure of Lionel Hampton, in effect, the star of the movie—he begins and ends it—and the true Mr. Rock and Roll.) Like Sinatra himself, jazz had grown from its saloon origins to become both typical and representative of America:

> And good or bad, [jazz] causes millions of people outside the United States to believe that we are by no means as crude, mysterious or childish as our foreign policy or its representatives have more often than not caused them to believe. And for that reason alone we should treat it and its makers with constant respect and

admiration. That aspect of it to which I contribute is also a considerable force for good in that tasteful songs and musically competent orchestral backgrounds, whether the words are understood or not, help keep the door open.

But the defense of jazz—which in the 1910s and 1920s was called by many status quo critics "crude, mysterious, and childish"—comes at the expense of Rock and Roll, which Sinatra calls

> . . . the most brutal, ugly, degenerate, vicious form of expression it has been my displeasure to hear. . . . It fosters almost totally negative and destructive reactions in young people. It smells phony and false. It is sung, played and written for the most part by cretinous goons and by means of its almost imbecilic reiterations and sly, lewd, in fact plain dirty—lyrics . . . it manages to be the martial music of every sideburned delinquent on the face of the earth.

The obvious reference at the end to Elvis Presley, Sinatra's main rival in popular music from 1956 through the end of that decade (Presley had fifteen number-one pop hits between 1956 and 1960), is not simply overwrought or excessively rehearsed; it is specifically generated by twin, conflicting urges in Sinatra: First, he uses the maniacal rhetoric of stigma and ridicule that historically had been used against Italians. ("Cretinous goons" and "most brutal, ugly, degenerate, vicious," were common descriptions of Italian gangsters and organized crime figures; "imbecilic reiterations" are suggestive of the implicit ridicule of Italian gestures and Pidgin English; even the "sideburned delinquent" conjures images of the "greaseball" with olive oil in his hair.) Second, the overheated critical language is nearly identical with that used to discredit ragtime at the turn of the century, jazz in its early days in the teens and twenties, and swing music of the thirties (Goodman at Carnegie Hall in 1938 was revolutionary)[4]—musical forms that overturned prevailing notions and traditions in American popular music, which changed American popular dance, and which were rooted in African-American musical expression.

Sinatra was using the invectives that had once been directed at him as an Italian, an outcast minority, and as a product of swing music, a discredited art form, to denounce a new music he felt was about to displace him. His was the conservative's cry for standards—literally, in this case, as that is what the body of so-called "timeless" pop songs is called—by using the language of degradation and contempt that reveals nothing more tellingly than that the oppressed wish access to the measure of respectability and acceptance that will permit them the luxury of defending the status quo. Sinatra, the rebel against the Hollywood establishment, was really defending its virtues and values as the shaper—through film, radio, records, and music publishing by means of which the studios exercised their power in music—of the public's taste in popular music. But when Hollywood began making youth films and Presley films in the mid-1950s, it seemed no longer the bulwark against the mass infantilism and bad taste that was early Rock and Roll, according to many contemporary critics. It is no wonder he gathered the Clan—the family of Hollywood outsiders —to make *Ocean's 11,* a last psycho-swing for masscult order and hipster resistance to another relentless surge of barbaric darkness in American life.

In 1959, the television series "The Untouchables" debuted much to the chagrin and displeasure of Sinatra and many other Italians, as they felt the show was defaming in its depiction of Prohibition-era Italian gangsters. Also in 1959, the federal government was investigating payola in radio air play, which resulted in the downfall of one popular Rock and Roll disc jockey, Alan Freed, but which also led to more insinuations about Italian gangsters in the pop music business. Earlier in the 1950s, a young Justice Department lawyer named Robert Kennedy had conducted an investigation of the teamsters' union and Jimmy Hoffa, which led to connections with organized crime and Italian gangsters. Boxing had also been investigated in the late 1950s, and while this exposure led to the downfall of the wealthy James Norris and his International Boxing Club, it also revealed that two Italian gangsters, Blinky Palermo and Frankie Carbo, were the masterminds behind restraint of trade and fixed fights in the boxing world.

Alan Freed's aforementioned self-serving and self-mythologizing 1957 film, *Mister Rock and Roll,* is about the rise of Teddy Randazzo, an Italian kid from New York, drawn to black Rhythm and Blues, who becomes a Rock and Roll singer, attracted to its sense of community, with Alan Freed as the father, as well to its aesthetics, but who is attacked in the respectable press for being a "delinquent" and a "troublemaker" through his music. Before Rock and Roll, he had worked as a bellhop in a Cleveland hotel. Alan Freed saved him from a life of working-class anonymity by bringing him together with the other unwanteds: the blacks, both eastern and midwestern, southern hillbilly whites, Jewish novelty songwriters, the urban working-class white girl destined for secretaryhood, all of whom make up his Rock and Roll shows. (The stereotypical attack against the Italian singer as a representative of his generation is not unlike the stereotypical attack made against black youths today and the music they are most identified with, Rap: "delinquents," "troublemakers," "degenerates," "gangsters.")[5] Ultimately, he and the girl reporter—who looks a great deal like Grace Kelly, the blonde WASP princess every ethnic male desires, and who inadvertently is responsible for this attack—become lovers, and Rock and Roll succeeds against its reactionary critics. Miscegenation proceeds at its lightning pace, and the East Coast white ethnic is as much at the center as the white southern boy. Oddly, the Italian, through his own ethnic darkness as well as his association with the black, becomes a strange figure of race mixing in America. Their own working-class fear of black competition in the job market and absorption of American racism made the Italians intensely anti-Negro, yet the Italian seems just a little better than a black, in the end. In passing, it is interesting to note one of the oddities of the American stage, the casting of a light-skinned black actor named Frank Silvera (who passed as a swarthy white but who, on several occasions, also played black roles) as the father of Italian actors Ben Gazzara and Tony Franciosa in *A Hatful of Rain.*

Sinatra was probably ambivalent about race mixing, supposedly having discouraged Sammy Davis, Jr., from marrying Kim Novak, with whom Davis had a love affair, but supporting him in his 1960 marriage to Swedish actress May Britt (a storm that Davis, with Sinatra's support, was able to weather a great deal better than Chubby Checker, the twist king, who, a few years later married a Scandinavian beauty queen and instantly disappeared from the charts). But Sinatra constantly made tasteless jokes about Sammy Davis's race and his interracial marriage during his 1960s stage act. The Italians had their Mafias, their Clans, their fixation on family, and their own fears of miscegenation, all of which made them so tribal. (While Sinatra had his Rat Pack, he also enjoyed tremendously the company of Italian gangsters and tough guys, a community which provided him, doubtless, with fantasy discharges about his masculinity and his ethnicity.) Perhaps Sinatra's ambiguity as Italian and aging pop singer was getting confused with and confronted by Rock and Roll's insistent myth of family togetherness.

Black Paternalism

In 1959, Berry Gordy, Jr., age 30, was forming his record company, Motown, or more precisely, Hitsville, U.S.A., in Detroit, built, at this early stage, primarily on the singing and songwriting strength of William "Smokey" Robinson, age 19, 1957 graduate of Northern High School, and Robinson's group, the Matadors, whom Gordy renamed the Miracles. (Robinson was always to hold a privileged position with the company. In the 1960s, he was the only performer who was permitted to write songs and produce recordings. He was also the only performer in the company's history to become a corporate executive.) The establishment of Motown was the beginning of a new family myth in popular culture, a myth that Motown has promoted and exploited for its entire history and has featured as a prominent part of its legacy. The 1985 film *The Big Chill*, which used Motown music as its soundtrack, was not only a sort of nostalgic memoir of a new "lost generation" but a coming together of people at a location to form a family. Virtually no major company in American history and surely no black company was ever so identified not simply as a family business but as a "family" enterprise for its employees; certainly, no independent record company was ever to manipulate so skillfully its humble, homemade origins as a mark of its distinction, its success, its power as a symbol in American culture in the way Motown has.

"By the time we returned in the winter of 1960, Motown was firmly established and running very much like family. Loyalty, honesty, and obedience were demanded and often gladly given," writes Mary Wilson of the Supremes in her autobiography, *Dream Girl*.

"Joining Motown was more like being adopted by a big loving family than being hired by a company," writes Otis Williams of the Temptations in his autobiography, *Temptations*.

"In the early days we were a family . . . we had so many good times together. We had picnics, Christmas parties, or we just hung out," said session pianist Earl Van Dyke, one of the numerous architects of the so-called Motown sound.

Martha Reeves, in her autobiography, *Dancing In the Street*, confirms: "Whenever Motown was called 'a family operation,' the reference to family was accurate. [Berry Gordy's] parents, 'Mom' and 'Pops' Gordy, as we lovingly called them, treated us all as their own. . . . They would both dress up and look so distinguished as they appeared at our openings, sending flowers, telegrams, and wishing us luck."

Gordy himself, finally, adds his bit to this "family" business in the foreword of the 1990 *The Motown Album* (the pun on the word "album" is both obvious and telling, as this scrapbook about the history of the record company is meant to suggest a family album of candid photos). Writes Gordy:

> Our loyalty to one another and to our goals was so strong that the only reasonable description of that energy was something beyond business and beyond contracts—it was the sticking together that only happens in families. . . .
> Though we did not coin the term ourselves, the "Motown Family" was not a description any of us took lightly. It was how other people described us, because it was the impression we gave other people. It doesn't matter what really accounted for our being perceived as a family, but I can tell you we all believed that we were. We certainly fought and loved like one.

The family myth resonated in two ways for Motown: First, as applied to an ostensibly black family, the Motown myth was particularly pleasing to blacks for whom "family" and "unity" are nearly fetishistic affections and affectations fraught with political and metaphysical meaning generated by a memory (nay, consciousness) of oppression. Nothing so warms the heart of the average African-American than an acknowledgment—philistine and sentimental as the current spate of Afrocentric greeting cards or gripping and compelling as John Wideman's memoirs—of the wondrous necessity of family. It must be remembered that in 1959, the year

Motown started, Lorraine Hansberry's play about black family life, *A Raisin in the Sun,* burst upon the scene. That play, which combines the worst of a Hallmark greeting card with the best of Russian drama, has endured as well as Motown's music. Second, the family myth meant that Berry Gordy was not merely a CEO, a boss, a leader, or even a visionary but that he was a father, an older brother, an uncle, a coach, a teacher, a guardian, an authority figure motivated by something other than making money from his acts. And the acts, of course, became his children, his brothers and sisters, his wards, his companions and not simply his employees.

This intense paternalism (Gordy's favorite phrase to his sometimes distraught and disgruntled artists was, "I'll take care of you") probably helped the company to survive in its early years. The bitterness and anger expressed in interviews and books by some former Motown artists and employees about their treatment at the company has largely been exacerbated or intensified by what some felt was a myth that was nothing more than self-serving hypocrisy. In short, the paternalism of the early years, and the implicit sense of racial uplift and "community"—fostered by the company's own bourgeois-motivated and practically rendered need in a racist society to have an identity of virtue and racial "commitment"—undoubtedly fostered the sense among many that Motown was not a privately owned enterprise which, in fact, it was, but some sort of cooperative venture. For a time, Gordy was able to manipulate bril-

liantly both his black and his white audiences by having
Motown as vaguely a "race company" satisfy certain nationalistic yearnings for blacks while presenting it as an
"assimilationist success story" for whites. He balanced,
through his family image, the neurotic need of his black
audience for uplift and the equally neurotic need for ac-
commodationist outreach for his white audience.

Part of the family myth was established by the inescapable fact that the company was literally family-run:
"Fuller, Esther, Anna, Loucye, George, Gwen, and
Robert all worked at Motown along with Mother and
Pop. You could find a Gordy lurking in practically every
department," writes Berry Gordy. "My own family was
and is close," writes Smokey Robinson in his autobiography, *Inside My Life,* "but I'd never seen anything like the
Gordys—four sisters and four brothers who made it
clear to their lovers and spouses and anyone else that
their family came first. The Gordys took care of business, but mainly they took care of each other." The myth
of family capitalism was important for Motown, despite
the fact that Gordy was unable, as it turned out, to pass
the company on to his children, because, in the disrep-
utable business of popular music-making, it gave him
the imprimatur of something established, linking, as it
were, clan and property or, more properly, in this instance, clan and technic. What is surprising, in an age
where, as Daniel Bell pointed out, "the old relation between the two institutions of property and family . . . has
broken down," is not that the myth of family capitalism

eventually petered out for Motown but that it managed to serve the company for as long as it did and is now a permanent part of the company's image. Motown was, ultimately, built as much on the powerful myth of Gordy's own family as on the myth of "family happiness" he projected and nurtured among his employees, and some explanation of the values that shaped this extraordinary family will help us to understand this extraordinary man.

A Usable Black Present
or the Lessons of Booker T. Washington
and Joe Louis

"Now, look here, Ellen," said Mr. Walters. (He called
her Ellen, for he had been long intimate with the family.)
"If you can't get on without the boy's earning something,
why don't you do as white women and men do? Do you
ever find them sending their boys out as servants? No;
they rather give them a stock of matches, blacking,
newspapers, or apples, and start them out to sell them.
What is the result? The boy that learns to sell matches
soon learns to sell other things; he learns to make
bargains; he becomes a small trader, then a merchant,
then a millionaire. Did you ever hear of any one who had
made a fortune at service?"

—Frank J. Webb's *The Garies and Their Friends* (1857), an
early African-American novel

My objections are, to our glorying and being happy in
such low employments; for if we are men, we ought to be
thankful to the Lord for the past, and for the future. Be
looking forward with thankful hearts to higher

attainments than wielding the razor and cleaning boots
and shoes.

—David Walker's *Appeal to the Colored Citizens of the
World*

Is it un-American for us to build our own homes, and
schools, hospitals and factories while we are suffering
and being turned away from many of yours? . . .
Is it un-American for us to build up an economic system
among ourselves?

—Elijah Muhammad's *Message to the Blackman in
America* (1965)

Since the black bourgeoisie live largely in a world of
make-believe, the masks which they wear to play their
sorry roles conceal the feelings of inferiority and of
insecurity and the frustrations that haunt their inner lives.

—E. Franklin Frazier's *Black Bourgeoisie* (1957)

How To Build A Nation

James Brown's 1974 "Funky President (People It's Bad)"
was, in its way, a more explicitly racial song than earlier
tunes like "King Heroin" (1972) or "Say It Loud—I'm
Black and I'm Proud" (1968). (And in this song, inci-
dentally, "bad" has no hip ironic meaning in black code.
It denotes precisely what it does in the mainstream.)
Perhaps that is why the tune was a hot black radio hit but
did only moderately well on the white pop charts.

"Funky President" harkened back to tunes like "Don't Be A Dropout" (1966), "I Don't Want Nobody To Give Me Nothing (Open the Door, I'll Get It Myself)" (1969), and "Get Up, Get Into It and Get Involved" (1970). All of these message songs could be called black songs of middle-class aspiration, in their own way, songs of working-class origin (and decided working-class appeal) that envisioned a black middle-brow nationalist world of self-reliance, faith in oneself, civic responsibility, and engagement. "Funky President"—the title itself being a satiric oxymoron, made for the occasion of Gerald Ford's becoming president after the Nixon resignation—has the same message except that it is couched, with some degree of soulfully rendered urgency, in the language of blacks owning businesses, controlling their community, saving their money ("like the mob," Brown sings, thus, another Italian connection). The song suggests, as the matter always has been in the African-American cultural vision, that the imminent demise of the black (since the days of slavery the African-American has never seen his situation here except in the most dire and perilous terms of precarious survival) is coupled with how much and how quickly he can adopt certain middle-class habits of morality and ingenuity.

One is struck by how at odds this remedy of rectitude and cunning bourgeois thrift may seem in relation to the desperation of the problem being addressed, just as it may be odd that a message of self-discipline and self-advancement should be so sincerely presented in a music that was considered by the mainstream, white culture such an attack on those very bourgeois, Christian values. E. Franklin Frazier, in his *Black Bourgeoisie* (1957), suggested that black business enterprise as a "social myth has been one of the main elements in the world of 'make-believe' which the black bourgeoisie has created to compensate for its feeling of inferiority in a white world dominated by business enterprise." A song such as "Funky President" and a good deal of James Brown's repertoire (a song like "It's a Man's World" or "It's a Man's, Man's, Man's World," cut in 1964, certainly suggests that Brown saw masculinity tied to material achievements and capitalist well-being) counters Frazier's view by proffering, first, that the black fantasy about black-owned business was something more than a middle-class make-believe, that is, a general make-believe of the race, if Brown's popularity as an artist is any indication; and second, that although this view of business may have been a sign of inferiority, it was also a sign of secular or profane aspiration for a subjugated people that may be as noble in its reach as it is tragic in some aspects of its unreality or shallowness. Perhaps this is one of the points that Zora Neale Hurston was trying to make with Joe Starks and Logan Killicks, two different types of male aspirants for bourgeois respectability, in her 1937 novel, *Their Eyes Were Watching God*. It meant a great deal to his black fans when James Brown became the first black performer to buy a Lear Jet, buy radio stations, cut deals with record companies, control entirely his stage show, and act, finally, as the complete and magisterial *auteur* of his own business mission as if, as a business property, he had sprung fully from his own imagination. For a people who feel that their history, in part, is and has been a long line of business abuses and humiliations and thefts on the part of whites, Brown's stature as musician/businessman and as conveyor of middle-class ambition is of no small measure. (The complexity of the myth of entrepreneurship and the meaning of business among African- Americans is something that Nelson George, in his provocative and often insightful book, *The Death of Rhythm and Blues,* seems to oversimplify entirely when he suggests that "[the] rejection of [Booker T.] Washington and the rise of the NAACP meant that the drive to assimilation became the dominant item on the black agenda. . . . Only a minority of blacks would openly agitate for more self-sufficiency." The drive to have businesses and to worship money culture—which Du Bois so eloquently warned against in his 1903 classic, *The Souls of Black Folk,* which George seems to have only selectively read—was a blatant attempt, despite its nationalistic pretensions, to assimilate or a proof of having assimilated!)[6]

"Funky President" was clearly a song that one could hardly imagine any white rock or country artist making or white audience consider interesting, as the American Dream of success is contextualized a bit differently for whites. Their assumptions about it and their cynicism over its emptiness tend not to match black assumptions and cynicism but to run parallel to them, as these assumptions and cynicism represent two distinct forms of a common nationalist mythology. This is largely because blacks and whites tend to see the community and the individual in almost oppositional ways: The white sees the individual's empowerment as a safeguard against the community's tyranny; blacks see the community's empowerment as the safeguard of the individual's dignity and fate. For many blacks, the song probably brought an image of the Nation of Islam and Elijah Muhammad's insistent "Do For Self" message, the current avatar of nationalism and self-respect through empire-building at the time the song was made, although such thinking predates the Black Muslims. Indeed, the Muslims were able to generate a certain regard and esteem from the African-American community because it preached a line that resonated in such a densely emotional way in those quarters. The dream of blacks owning business, being liberated through entrepreneurship, is not new. James Brown himself exploited the image of being a successful businessman in the 1960s and 1970s, although like Elijah Muhammad, his commercial kingdom was less than puffed up to be and disappeared fairly quickly. We might understand Berry Gordy and the making of Motown by understanding that the connections between commerce, the virtue of accumulating wealth, and African-American life and culture are deep, intricate, remarkably philistine, and silly, as E. Franklin has suggested, yet remarkably compelling.

Young Man Gordy and the Making of Americans

When Berry Gordy, Sr.—one of the many black southern immigrants who came north during the Great Migration of the 1920s—moved his business from a rented location to his own building on the east side of Detroit, his wife, Bertha, a schoolteacher, named it the Booker T. Washington Grocery Store and, thus, paid tribute not only to one of the most important black leaders of the 20th century but to a set of values and be liefs, aspirations and morals, that coalesced around Washington but were expressed far earlier in African-American history by such disparate 19th century black leaders and writers as Paul Cuffe, Frederick Douglass, Richard Allen, James Forten, Martin Delany, William Wells Brown, and David Walker, each of whom had entrepreneurial enterprises of varying kinds, from churches (the major business endeavor in the black community) to newspapers to sail-making to writing. Interestingly, even the men listed here who were ex-slaves are not seen in historical hindsight as southerners but rather as northern black abolitionists. This last is no insignificant point, as shall be seen in discussing Booker T. Washington. If there has been a myth of white American energy and enterprise that is generated by a history of national expansion, there has been a corresponding mythical urge of black American nationhood built on the notions of black energy and self-sufficiency, an urge to separation stimulated by the African-Americans' history of segregation and an urge to achievement fueled by America's own preoccupation with success and ambition and blacks' need to disprove their perceived and storied inferiority.

Booker T. Washington, the figurehead and secular institution builder around whom this urge to black nationhood has received its most ironic articulation, was, in some sense, never really a southerner. In his autobiography, *Up From Slavery* (1901), he informs his reader that his models were Mrs. Viola Ruffner and General S. C. Armstrong, both white northerners. His accounts of his labors in a West Virginia salt mine, his supervision of Indian students at Hampton, and his teaching school back in West Virginia give his early life more of a middle-western than a southern flavor. When the Gordys, called their establishment the Booker T. Washington Grocery Store, it was these very qualities, these signatures of bourgeois rectitude—thrift, Yankee ingenuity, hard work, business acumen, ambition, willingness to do humble, menial work—associated with both the North and the West and championed by Washington that were being commemorated. (And as Berry Gordy, Jr. makes clear in his autobiography, *To Be Loved,* his parents worked very hard to inculcate those values in their large brood.) Washington may have preached to blacks over and over to stay in the South, but a book like *Up From Slavery* makes clear that he was warning them against being southerners by habit.

Few families practiced more fervently or more successfully the success ethic of Booker T. Washington than the Gordys. Berry "Pops" Gordy, Sr.'s father, Berry Gordy, was a highly successful businessman and landowner, and a meticulous record keeper in post–Civil War Georgia, and when the father died tragically during a lightning storm, Pops continued in his father's footsteps: "I always had money; I had money all the time," Pop writes, or more properly recites, in his oral autobiography. Indeed, his success—farming, running a produce and meat business—led to his being forced from Georgia because he had too much money for a black man in the South in those days to be able to avoid coming to a bad end at the hands of jealous whites. In Detroit, he worked as a plasterer, a grocer, and eventually as a printer, and he employed his eight children in his enterprises and taught them the Washingtonian virtues of petit bourgeois success. This, of course, set the precedent for having the family work at Motown for son, Berry, Jr. (In his autobiography, Berry, Jr. suggests that he often found his father's passion for hard work an expression of inefficiency, his father also made several bad or disadvantageous business deals, partly because of his mania for work. Gordy gives two vivid, if brief, examples of how he learned the craft of business dealing by watching Jews.)

Surprisingly for a family with such bourgeois aspirations, Berry Gordy, Jr., as an adolescent and young adult, tried to be a professional boxing champion, a pursuit one would normally associate with the scion of a more economically depressed household. But there were two ma-

jor reasons for Gordy's boxing ambitions: First, Gordy
was born in Detroit in 1929 and grew up during the era
of Joe Louis, whose family came from Alabama to
Detroit roughly four or so years after the Gordys. (Sugar
Ray Robinson, the boxing wunderkind, who was born in
Detroit in 1921 but grew up in New York, was also
an influence as he and Gordy were closer in weight.
Robinson's family had migrated from a farm in
Georgia.) Louis was more than a boxer, more than a
champion athlete; he was the personification of a broad
and compelling black triumph, a symbol of black freedom, assertion, and achievement during an age when
blacks experienced rigid segregation and were beginning
to become restive about their prolonged degradation and
disenfranchisement, and during an age when the heavyweight championship was the most coveted title in all of
sports. Louis won the championship in 1937 when
Gordy was eight and retired in 1949 when Gordy was
twenty. Louis was Gordy's first and probably most impressive hero, a homeboy who made impossibly good.
As Gordy, Jr. writes about the time of Louis's 1938 victory over Max Schmeling: "I was only eight at the time,
but I knew Joe Louis was a hero, a hero of all the people,
but he was black like me. I knew what that meant. Even
at eight years old I had gotten a taste of the world—the
real world—the white world." Second, Gordy grew up
during the Depression when a greater number of boys
from working-class, petit-bourgeois, and blue-collar
backgrounds (Barney Ross, a Jew, whose father was also

a merchant, comes to mind right away) went into the sport as it offered far more money for success than other professional sports during a time when even lower middle-class families were strapped. It was moreover the only professional sport where a black might be able to cash in big. Boxing in the 1930s and 1940s was more a sport for working-class boys than it is today when most of its participants are from what is called the underclass.

Gordy was a decent boxer as both an amateur and a professional but he fought in too light a weight classification—bantamweight and, later, a featherweight—to make much money unless he could do something spectacular like Henry Armstrong and win titles in several weight divisions simultaneously. Apparently, Gordy was not *that* good. His ambition to be a champion boxer in a lighter weight division, however, was not completely unrealistic or unreasonable; during his boyhood, Gordy knew that such lighter weight fighters—that is, divisions below middleweight—as Armstrong, Ross, Lou Ambers, Tony Canzoneri, Jimmy McLarin, and Kid Chocolate had made names for themselves and decent amounts of cash. The failed boxing career affected Gordy in two ways: First, because he quit school in the 11th grade to pursue boxing, Gordy never learned to read or write very well (although he did receive his GED while in the service), which meant, in the end, that Gordy became an intuitive intelligence, something that actually stood him in good stead in the game of trying to anticipate and predict hit records. Second, he learned that in any career pursuit the risks one takes must be balanced by the possibilities of the rewards if the risks are successfully negotiated. He discovered in boxing that the risks he endured as a fighter far exceeded the rewards he might enjoy, even if he became a champion. He eventually decided to gamble on music (something he had always been interested in) because the risks seemed more reasonable and the rewards more fulfilling. Gordy describes his departure from boxing in this way: "Then, one hot August day in 1950, a remarkable thing happened. . . . As I sat down on a bench, my eyes fell on two posters on one of the four square pillars that supported the gym's ceiling. . . .

"The top poster announced a Battle of the Bands between Stan Kenton and Duke Ellington for that same night. The one below was advertising a bout between two young fighters. . . .

"I stared at both posters for some time, realizing the fighters could fight once and maybe not fight again for three or four weeks, or months, or never. The bands were doing it every night, city after city, and not getting hurt. I then noticed the fighters were about twenty-three and looked fifty; the band leaders about fifty and looked twenty-three."

The conjunction in Gordy, Jr. of the Washingtonian practices absorbed from his father and the experience of Joe Louis's heroism meant that he could use the example of, arguably, the two most important and influential pre-1950s black leaders: the "realistic" virtues of the petit-bourgeois habits of industry and tenacity espoused by

Washington and the "idealistic" possibility of an extravagant impact on American popular culture at large à la Joe Louis. It must be remembered that both Louis and Washington, despite the "nationalistic" renderings given them by many blacks, were, in essence, crossover heroes; it was Louis who was cheered, even celebrated, by whites for beating white opponents, something that was unthinkable during the reign of the first black heavyweight champion, Jack Johnson (1908–1915). Louis also became one of the major idols of World War II, a first in American popular culture. It was Washington who ate dinner at the White House with Roosevelt (a striking icon, as many of the civil-disobedience confrontations during the civil rights era occurred at eating places), who extolled white hero figures, and who suggested that blacks could, too, adopt the values of white Protestant America. Both the ideas of a usable black male heroism and of a crossover appeal to whites as well as high-class blacks—two models steeped paradoxically in the contrary worlds of straight-laced middleclass respectability and the larger-than-life, street-corner world of masculine derring-do—would have enormous and obvious effect on Gordy, Jr., in creating his vision for Motown. In combining the lessons from Louis and Washington, Gordy, indirectly and inadvertently, learned something from the other major black figure of the century, W.E.B. Du Bois. It was Du Bois in his famous remark about black double-consciousness in his seminal *The Souls of Black Folk* who said:

The history of the American Negro is the history of this strife—this longing to attain self-conscious manhood, to merge his double self into a better and truer self. In this merging he wishes neither of the older selves to be lost. He would not Africanize America, for America has too much to teach the world and Africa. He would not bleach his Negro soul in a flood of white Americanism, for he knows that Negro blood has a message for the world. He simply wishes to make it possible for a man to be both a Negro and an American. . . ."

As Du Bois suggests, a black can be neither just a Negro (that is, exist purely and solely on the basis of his racial consciousness), nor can he be just an American (that is, exist purely and solely on the plane of a national, nonracial, mythic consciousness) without, in either case, losing a vital dimension of his identity. Gordy, from the examples of Washington and Louis, in essence, learned how to merge the identities of being black and being American and this merging was key to the formation and success of Motown. Gordy, with the music he was to create, pinpointed, as did Du Bois, the precise identity neurosis of both blacks and whites: the African-American's fear that he will be bleached into whiteness and the white's fear that he will be Africanized. The one fears the tragedy of being a mulatto, the other the degradation of being a mongrel. Gordy managed to negotiate these neuroses by appealing to American youth through music that neither bleached nor blackened, although, of course, from the margins, throughout his career, he was accused simultaneously of doing both.

After an uneventful if unsatisfying stint in the army[7] (unlike Pops, Gordy, Jr., was unable to contrive an early discharge), Gordy, like most young people in search of themselves and a career, went through a series of jobs during the fifties, but in this case they fortunately prepared him for the career culmination as head of his own recording company. Initially, Gordy worked in the family's print shop or with the family's plastering business, doing back-breaking work in either instance. As Nelson George writes in his book on Motown, *Where Did Our Love Go?*: "Pops wouldn't accept anything less than hard work from his boys. He believed in nepotism, but not as an excuse for inferior workmanship." In 1953, Gordy married Thelma Louise Coleman, and with a loan his father managed for him from the church credit union and his army discharge pay, Gordy started the 3-D Record Mart, a retail store that specialized in jazz records. "I was always a jazz lover," Gordy said later, "I loved Billie Holiday. In terms of other jazz people, I liked the ad-libbing ability, which is really another form of songwriting, of Charlie Parker or Sonny Stitt, Lester Young, Miles Davis, Thelonious Monk, Art Tatum." Gordy, something of a hipster, had been hanging out in the jazz scene in Detroit and thought he could turn his passion into a money-making venture. In two years the store closed because few Detroit blacks wanted to buy records by Charlie Parker and Lester Young, much preferring the leading performers of the Rhythm and Blues craze, Louis Jordan, Johnny Ace, Ivory Joe Hunter, LaVern Baker, and Faye Adams. As saxophonist Johnny Griffin said, the promoters "took [jazz] out of Harlem and put it in Carnegie Hall and downtown in those joints where you've got to be quiet. The black people split and went back to Harlem, back to the rhythm and blues, so they could have a good time." Oversimplified as an explanation, as David H. Rosenthal in his book, *Hard Bop*, asserts, but nonetheless, in broad measure, correct.

After the failure of the record store, Gordy, who had begun working at Ford's Wayne assembly plant and whose marriage was not in good shape (eventually he and his wife separated, but having three children merely intensified the pressure he felt to find some way to make money) began to hang around the fringes of the R and B world, passing himself off as a songwriter. With the help of his sisters, Anna and Gwen, who had secured—in typical Gordy go-getter fashion—the photography and cigarette concessions at the famous Flame Show Bar, Gordy was introduced to several musicians, including Maurice King and Thomas "Beans" Bowles, both of whom would eventually work for Motown (along with pianist Earl Van Dyke, bassist Jimmy Jamerson, and drummer Benny Benjamin, the rhythm section that would give Motown recordings their unique thrust), managers, hustlers, nightclub owners and other types who populated the subterrestrial world of black American popular music during the age of segregation. In 1957, Gordy, determined to be a full-time songwriter, began writing songs for another Detroit ex-fighter, Jackie Wilson, "Mr. Excitement" as he was called on the chit'ling circuit, who, along with Clyde McPhatter—both of whom came out of Billy Ward and his Dominoes—were among the most renowned R and B voices of their time. "In early 1957 music was literally everywhere," Gordy writes. "Now that music was my business, I wanted to be a part of all of it." Several of Gordy's songs, written for Wilson between 1957 and 1959 in partnership with Tyran Carlo, aka Roguel Billy Davis, became major hits: "Reet Petite" (Gordy's parody of Elvis Presley), "Lonely Teardrops," "To Be Loved," "I'll Be Satisfied," and "That's Why I Love You So." Gordy realized little money from these hits, as royalties for songwriters took a long time to materialize, and in the free-and-easy world of R and B were not likely to be paid completely. Moreover, Gordy did not publish his own tunes at this time, which meant he was at the mercy of the music publisher and the record company Wilson recorded for to give accounts of sales, something he was just not likely to get from them.

In 1958 Gordy met Raynoma Liles, a trained musician with perfect pitch, who was to become his second wife. She encouraged him to produce records—that is, take responsibility for a song's arrangements, harmonies, mixes, and the overall structure and presentation of a record—a move that eventually led to the formation of Hitsville, or Motown Records. Within a year, he had scored a medium hit with Marv Johnson's "Come to

Me" and a major hit with Barrett Strong's "Money (That's What I Want)," the former recorded at the famous Hitsville building on West Grand Boulevard, the latter on his own Tamla label, and had discovered a teenaged group—Smokey Robinson and the Miracles—that could deliver his sound to a young audience. His initial capital came from an $800 loan from the Gordy family kitty, Ber-Berry Co-op. He knew right away that he wanted to run his own company. In 1961, Gwen married Harvey Fuqua, the former lead singer of the Moonglows and the man responsible for bringing Marvin Gaye to Detroit, who resurrected Anna's company through his own, Harvey and Tri-Phi Records, forming Anna-Tri Phi. These companies were soon bought out by Berry Gordy. They provided him with the Spinners, Shorty Long, Junior Walker and the All-Stars, and (probably most important) a singer named Lamont Anthony, who, under the name of Lamont Dozier, became part of the famous Holland, Dozier, and Holland songwriting team at Motown. With the arrival in 1960 of street-wise William "Mickey" Stevenson, the first of a series of "hot," richly creative record producers, the pieces were in place. Motown was born.

Reviewing Gordy's career up to the founding of Motown, it is clear how each of his missteps helped him ultimately. The 3-D Record Mart failed not simply because Gordy was selling the wrong product; he switched his stock to what his patrons were buying, but the store still failed. Somehow, this early on, Gordy had little in-

terest in, or his temperament had little tolerance for, being a petit-bourgeois merchant. He somehow wanted to
shape and influence taste and music and not merely supply a product to fulfill a need. He decided to reorient his
listening habits and his taste to the new sound of R and B
because he realized that this potentially was new cutting-
edge music. Presumably, he was regularly reading
Billboard (virtually every record-store owner did and
does), the magazine of charts and trends in the record industry, during his years as a record-store owner, and he
certainly would have noted the issue devoted entirely to
R and B published on April 24, 1954, or articles such as
one entitled "Death Certificate Premature: R and B
Ain't Ever Been Sick" in the July 25, 1955, issue. Finally,
from the record store, he learned about record distribution and how records can be best marketed for the public
and precisely what publics exist for which records.

His job at the Ford plant, as Nelson George and
other critics have pointed out, made him aware of two
things: how production can be efficiently organized and
automated for the highest quality. At Motown during
the sixties, producers could also write songs and songwriters could produce, but artists—either singers or session musicians—were not permitted to do either. With
this type of control, Motown put out a highly consistent
product. It was in the 1970s when the artist became both
producer and writer—in short, when the album became
a "work" in black music and the artist became an
auteur—that Motown faltered, as Gordy was uncom-

fortable with that trend. His disagreements with Stevie Wonder, Marvin Gaye, Diana Ross, and the Jackson 5 over this point are well known. From his auto plant experience, Gordy also became aware that to keep his company going, it was necessary to provide a series of attractive rewards and incentives for hard work, as well as an elaborate system of shaming for laziness. A record company, like an auto company, requires an almost unbearable atmosphere of competition. Gordy believed in competition with the fervor of a fanatic. (This intense sense of contest not only created a celebrity system within the company but became a point of celebration about the company, a virtual mark of internal and external prestige.) Thus, producers with hit records at Motown were given more studio time, and the others had to fight for what was left. The hottest songwriters were allowed to work with the hottest singers. At company meetings, Gordy bluntly criticized any song or performance he considered inferior, not permitting the song to be released, thereby angering his producers and songwriters, but also spurring them to do better in order to curry his favor and approval. This system produced an unprecedented number of hit records in relation to the number of records released. Gordy also learned how the wave of the future was the tinny-sounding car radio, where most young people were first to hear new records. Motown records were always mixed to sound well coming over car radios. Finally, the Ford job taught him that he could not accept anonymous menial work under a stranger's direction. He knew there was absolutely no future in it. As Elliot Liebow perceptively points out in his classic work, *Tally's Corner*: ". . . the busboy or dishwasher who works hard becomes, simply, a hard-working busboy or dishwasher." Or assembly-line worker, in the case of Gordy.

His work as a songwriter introduced him to one essentially creative phase of the production of mass-directed popular music, and from it he learned how songs are put together and how they are recorded. Gordy was musically illiterate; he could neither play an instrument (he can doodle on the piano by ear and play what is called "arranger's chords") nor read music but he had a great sense of what constitutes a good pop-cum–R and B song, as both Raynoma Gordy Singleton and Smokey Robinson testify in their autobiographies. He was—like many others who came into popular music at this time, to use Alec Wilder's pejorative term—an "amateur." What frightens the trained musician is the idea that someone who is an "amateur" can make music successfully simply by understanding music not as an art, nor as a highly complex set of techniques or an elaboration of rules, but rather as a series of effects and gimmicks that can be manipulated by anyone with an ear and some imagination. What angered traditionalists was that the coming of people like Gordy was, in effect, the deconstruction of popular music, the explosion of it as a contrivance and a strategy and not the continued reverence for it as an artistry and a craft. Pop traditionalists feared that Rock and Roll was not merely formula—that was acceptable—but was illusion, a parlor trick that mocked music itself. In an age when many feared the manipulative powers of a burgeoning mass culture apparatus, from C. Wright Mills on the left to Whittaker Chambers on the right, such a response was hardly surprising. Gordy's rules for songs were simple but effective: Always use the present tense; never overdo the hook; make sure the song has a hummable melody, which means that it should be like something the public's heard before; find originality in the song's concept, in how its lyrics are phrased, in its rhythm. Like the young white songwriters and producers who reorganized Tin Pan Alley through overly orchestrated pop–Rhythm and Blues of the late 1950s and the early 1960s at the Brill Building or with what became known as the Brill Building Sound—Berry Mann and Cynthia Weil, Carole King and Gerry Goffin, Doc Pomus and Mort Shuman, and Leiber and Stoller who churned out songs for groups and singers like the Drifters, the Coasters, the Shirelles, Ray Charles, and Ben E. King—Gordy did not write songs, he wrote *records*. The point was for the singer to serve the song, and not the song the singer. It was a common practice, for instance, for producers Mickey Stevenson and Brian Holland to use additional voices in mixing the recordings of the Marvelettes, one of Motown's successful girl groups, to make them sound smoother and fuller. The girls in the group, apparently, never knew this at the time.

Because additional voices, string orchestras, and

other effects were added to many Rock and Roll records, fans were often disappointed when they heard these groups and singers perform in person. Unlike jazz artists whose "live" performances were expected to exceed their recordings, Rock and Roll performers were often a great deal less in person than their records. This is why James Brown's first *Live at the Apollo Theater* album, recorded in 1962, was such an epochal event in the history of Rock and Roll, as it proved, by becoming one of the best-selling R and B albums of that year, that some forms of this music could be captured live with great effect. It remains Brown's biggest-selling album, never yielded a hit single, and reached number two on the pop charts in the summer of 1963. At this time, of course, live recordings in jazz were routine, with most major artists having one or more such recordings to their credit. Motown, with even more daring innovation, scored a big hit in 1963 with a live single of Little Stevie Wonder, "Fingertips, Part 2," modeling the young artist after Ray Charles, who recorded a live album in 1959 that inspired Brown. This song launched Wonder's career. Motown thus helped to further the possibilities that at least some live Rock and Roll could be effectively recorded. Interestingly, these two records succeeded, in part, because they offered, like a jazz record, live instrumental prowess—in Brown's instance, his entire band, one of the best in post–World War II popular-music history, and in Wonder's instance, because of his solo harmonica playing. In effect, both Wonder and Brown were authentic auteurs with these records. Nonetheless, these exceptions only further prove the rule that Rock and Roll records were studio contrivances, and neither songwriters nor producers cared one whit how these performers sounded in person.

Gordy essentially had some of the same aesthetic principles as the Brill Building crowd but his sound lasted longer, was more encompassing—covering soul jazz–cum–R and B with the organ/sax combo of Junior Walker and the All-Stars, to the frantic parody of doo-wop with the Contours, to its reinvention as sophistication by the Temptations through the crossover combination of the Andrews Sisters, the Shirelles, and the Davis Sisters in the Supremes—and made an even bigger impact on the culture at large.

"Most Afro-Americans can't sing pop," said James Brown in his autobiography. "They may think they can, but they can't." While this may be true, it is almost equally true that if they cannot sing pop, they can be made to *appear* to sing it. Brown himself did this on such early songs as "Try Me," "Prisoner of Love," and the aforementioned "It's a Man's, Man's, Man's World," for he surely was no pop singer. If Brown's songs make the pop charts, however, then what is pop? Is it merely a technique that can be mimicked by anyone, a set of conventions and gestures that can be adapted by anyone with a sense of what the market likes? Or does pop music have an aesthetic of its own?

Among Motown's singers, only Diana Ross had a truly "pop" voice, that is, an absolutely depthless, completely synthetic voice, but Gordy found ways to make many of his singers seem pop. He changed the late Mary Wells from R and B to pop by making her singing less strident and less rooted in the black gospel tradition. On Wells's first record, "Bye Bye Baby," which she wrote, her voice is hoarse and harsh (partly owing to the number of takes), with intense melismatic flourishes and shouts, the sort of vocal ornamentation that would please a black church audience but might leave many whites indifferent. Once Smokey Robinson began to write for her, however, her style became softer, her voice relaxed and sweet, poignant and cute, and her lyrics adolescent.

Robinson's songwriting was essential to Motown's early success. He had a great ear for love lyrics that were familiar but not clichéd. But what made a great tune, say, out of the Temptations' "My Girl" was the tension between its rather sentimental words and the late David Ruffin's strong gospel-fueled voice, which threatened to break out of the song's pop sensibility at any second. (Ruffin was, along with Levi Stubbs of the Four Tops, Motown's most dramatic male voice.) Gordy, like the Brill producers, encouraged Robinson and his other songwriters to use this contrast. The idea was to give the pop audience a pop tune with a nonpop voice. Holland, Dozier, and Holland did this to great effect with their melodramatic, overwrought songs for the Four Tops.

Yet without a trained musician such as wife Raynoma as a trusted second who shared his vision, Gordy would have had greater difficulty getting the Motown

Sound off the ground. He needed someone who could write lead sheets for the musicians, who could make sure the background singers were performing in the proper harmony, and who could transpose keys if the original key of a song was inappropriate for the singer. But Gordy was not only a man of considerable talent and vision, he was also a person who could spot and exploit talent in someone else. Yet despite what Gordy brought to his own career, without certain historical and technological forces at work, Motown would never have been born.

The technological changes are easy to enumerate: the birth of the transistor, the long-playing album (33⅓ RPM) and the single (45 RPM) in the late 1940s, and the emergence of television as a mass-culture contraption in the 1950s. It is difficult to say whether these changes were the cause or the effect of the explosion of interest in music among the general public but, as Jacques Barzun points out, music had become, by the 1950s, "a passionate avocation," a change in attitude that "amounts to a cultural revolution." People grew more intensely interested in music not only once it became an artifact (commercial recording started in the 1910s) but also when it became ubiquitous through sound movies, radio, hi-fi, television, and the like, that is, once it became divorced from an actual live performance or occasion and could exist as a representation of itself. Moreover, in the 1950s—the age of the Cold War and intense ideological debates over the fate of the world, as well as intense scrutiny about the nature of political and intellectual commitment demanded from each citizen—music (because for the nonmusician it is nonintellectual, an escape from ideology and ideas) may have been especially attractive at this time, in the same way as becoming the hipster—Mailer's White Negro (many white Los Angeles teens were trying to become cholos as a sign of hipness)—to escape into some romanticized idealization of a racial minority's identity was another means of escape from the Cold War pressure of constricted and constrained identity options.

The effect of the invention of the transistor was similar to the later invention of the microchip: It made electronic appliances smaller and cheaper, particularly radios. In fact, it spurred the growth of portable radios, which had an enormous impact on where music was listened to and on the mating habits of people who used music on the radio for sensual purposes. The LP became the "adult" record of the market and the industry's best-selling format as well, since most recorded music was packaged in this way. (Sinatra, for instance, was the leading seller of LPs in the 1950s, and Columbia Records started their record club in 1955 geared to adults with LPs of pop, easy listening, jazz, and classical.) The 45 single became the format in which Rock and Roll was presented to the public. It was not until the late 1950s— the time of the emergence of Motown—that the 78 RPM was phased out of the R and B market. This was an important event as it signaled that black popular music and white popular music were available in the same format, making crossover easier. Rock and Roll and Rhythm and Blues were largely seen as "singles"—that is, 45 RPM music—it was not until well into the sixties that these forms began to exploit the album format as an artistic concept and not simply as repository of a few hit singles and a bunch of B sides. Finally, television was of major importance in the dissemination of the new youth and black popular musics, largely through such shows as Dick Clark's "American Bandstand," which later spawned "Shindig" and "Hullabaloo"—shows essential to Motown's success, which were simply rebuilt versions of "Your Hit Parade"—and older variety shows like the "Ed Sullivan Show," all of which gave an aura of respectability to black music by making it appear more mainstream.

Television was also the final kiss of death for jazz as a popular music. Because jazz was used so much as background music for TV shows in the 1950s, it became relegated in the public's mind to incidental or programmatic or, worse, mood music that was not meant to be listened to, with hardly a personality of its own. Moreover, for the youth of America and for many blacks, jazz became a kind of staid establishment music as a result of television's cooption and its own self-conscious intellectual pretensions. There were exceptions, such as the popularity of Henry Mancini's theme for the show, "Peter Gunn"; the cool jazz of Miles Davis and the Third Stream of Dave Brubeck and the Modern Jazz Quartet; the midsixties recordings of drummer Chico Hamilton that featured Memphis reedman Charles Lloyd, bassist Al Stinson, and Hungarian guitarist Gabor Szabo, which were considered especially hip among the black cogno-scenti; the piano stylings of Ahmad Jamal and Oscar Peterson; and, for the black masses particularly, the growth of organ-sax-guitar soul jazz combos: Jimmy Smith's, Brother Jack McDuff's, and Jimmy McGriff's, or the hard, gospel-tinged bop of Horace Silver and Cannonball Adderley that indicated a consuming preoc-cupation among blacks with presenting themselves artis-tically in complex, exaggerated poses as primitives in touch with a more spiritual core while being superb, if intimidating, technicians whose music could not be cov-ered by whites.

In this respect, the two most influential musicians for the African-American masses between 1955 and 1970—the two instrumentalists who were considered most deeply black—may very well have been organist Smith and Texas-born, honking tenor saxophonist and bandleader King Curtis (born Curtis Ousley), who led or participated in sessions at Enjoy, Scepter, Prestige, and Atlantic Records, among others, the last three being among the most important independent companies putting out popular black music during this period, the last specializing in Rhythm and Blues and jazz. Curtis, who was murdered in 1971, became an important pur-veyor of R and B, funk, soul jazz, and Memphis Soul, all the major areas of popular instrumental black music, from 1950 until his death. (The honking tenor saxes and the screaming Hammond B-3, the latter straight from the black church, never much appealed to whites, who thought the sound to be raucous and loud, with little artistic pretension or principle that made much sense to them. James Brown, however, successfully crossed over this aesthetic in his music, where his vocal style and band arrangements approximated the screams and honks of this style of jazz. In fact, in his autobiography, Brown said that he disliked the blues and saw his music as a form of jazz.) But generally jazz was being pushed off the scene as a popular force of the magnitude that it had been in the past.

The historical forces that helped make Motown possible are a bit more complex in their rendering. But one particular historical happening seems very clear: Just as Frank Sinatra saw the 1960 election of Kennedy as something portentous, as a signification of a new era (because, as many have said, he felt that he was delivering a president to his friend, Chicago mob chief Sam Giancana, who purportedly produced the 200,000 Chicago votes that provided the margin of victory), so too, for vastly different reasons, did Gordy. As Raynoma Gordy writes in her *Berry, Me, and Motown*:

> To Berry and to me, President John Fitzgerald Kennedy symbolized the idealism we shared—the belief that doors would open for us, that anything was possible. . . . It was an awe-inspiring time. JFK was new and

fresh, young and exciting. So was his wife. And *we* [Berry and I] were all those things. I'd look at their picture in the paper and think how romantic they were. Like us.

At no time in their history did blacks feel more optimistic about the future than in 1960 when things were changing, when a young president's rhetoric was promising so much and so richly, when a young black southern preacher was speaking so eloquently for a brave new humankind, and it was quite possible, at last, to think of entering the world of whites without going through the back door of the culture.

The Midwest as Musical
Mecca and the Rise of
Rhythm and Blues

Detroit was a real music town. You heard it everywhere, from radios and record players, outside the doors of the clubs that kids like us were too young to enter legally, from guys and girls standing out on the street singing. It sounds like a scene out of a musical, but that's truly how it was.

—Otis Williams, *Temptations*

Nowhere else in the nation and at no other time have blues musicians ever been more firmly dedicated to the proposition that it don't mean a thing if it ain't got that swing than in Kansas City in the early 1930s.

—Albert Murray, *Stomping the Blues*

It was in Chicago that "King Porter Stomp" was first recorded, by King Oliver in 1924. It was in Chicago that it was made popular by Benny Goodman, playing a Fletcher Henderson arrangement of it in 1936. And of course it had been in Chicago that black musicians had gathered together to share talent and ideas during the

Columbian Exposition of 1893—this looked forward to
Chicago's Century of Progress Fair of 1933, after which
that city became the most fertile ground for jazz, later
called "swing." Jazz was not of course conceived in
Chicago, but it was most certainly incubated there.

—Dempsey Travis, *An Autobiography of Black Jazz*

Writers both in and outside the region agreed that the
Middle West had replaced the East as the standard by
which to gauge other sections of the nation.

—James Shortridge on the heyday of the Middle West as
idealized American region in his *The Middle West: Its
Meaning in American Culture*

White and Black Middle West

"That's my Middle West," wrote F. Scott Fitzgerald
through the voice of narrator Nick Carraway toward the
end of his 1925 novel, *The Great Gatsby*, "not the wheat
or the prairies or the lost Swede towns, but the thrilling
returning trains of my youth, and the street lamps and
the sleigh bells in the frosty dark and the shadows of
holly wreaths thrown by lighted windows on the snow. I
am part of that, a little solemn with the feel of those long
winters, a little complacent from growing up in the
Carraway house in a city where dwellings are still called
through decades by a family's name."

But the snow and the houses of the middle-western

city struck Richard Wright's protagonist, Bigger Thomas, differently in the seminal 1940 novel, *Native Son*:

> As the car lurched over the snow [Bigger] lifted his eyes and saw black people upon the snow-covered sidewalks. Those people had feelings of fear and shame like his. Many a time he had stood on street corners with them and talked of white people as long sleek cars zoomed past. To Bigger and his kind white people were not really people; they were a sort of great natural force, like a stormy sky looming overhead, or like a deep swirling river stretching suddenly at one's feet in the dark. . . .
>
> After a few feet [Bigger] stopped and swung the light. He saw dusty walls, walls almost like those of the Dalton home. The doorways were wider than those of any house in which he had ever lived. Some rich white folks lived here once, he thought. Rich white folks. That was the way most houses on the South Side were, ornate, old, stinking; homes once of rich white people, now inhabited by Negroes or standing dark and empty with yawning black windows.

Fitzgerald, a white native midwesterner who came of age as a writer during a decade when several other mid-westerners—Sinclair Lewis, Glenway Wescott, Theodore Dreiser (who started before the others), and Sherwood Anderson—were examining midwestern life, might be expected to have a different view than Wright, a black native southerner, who came north to flee the intense segregation and racism of the South, only to be thwarted and embittered by the North's own version of segregation and racism. Even in earlier novels, such as Langston Hughes's *Not Without Laughter* (1930) or Jean Toomer's *Cane* (1924), where the Middle West is prominently featured as either big city or small town, in one case by a native midwesterner and in the other by a borderline southerner from Washington, D.C., it is perceived differently—not nearly so idyllically as Fitzgerald's, yet unambiguously better or at least decidedly different from the landscape of the Deep South. Even in some of the works of a more contemporary writer like Toni Morrison, *Sula* (1974) and *Song of Solomon* (1977), this is clearly true.

It is notable that blacks have always referred to the area of Kansas, Nebraska, and Oklahoma as "the territory," a designation implying both space, escape, and freedom that they never applied to any place in the South or along the northern Atlantic seaboard. As Alain Locke reminds us in his 1925 essay, "The New Negro," black southerners did not go to the North and West spurred simply by necessity but by the same hope for advancement and economic opportunity that moved Europeans to come to America in the late 19th century and earlier. (Interestingly, the premiere of "Amos 'N' Andy" on radio in 1925, destined to become the longest-running and most popular show in radio history, showcased for the first time in American popular culture, on a regular basis, a black community—albeit, created by two white men—in this instance, in Chicago, the heart of the Middle West.) That all did not turn out as African Americans would have liked does not diminish the fact that in the Middle West, blacks experienced greater freedom personally in many instances and clearly saw greater freedom among the whites (part of the mythic history of the Midwest is the value placed there on egalitarianism) than they witnessed in the South, and this, undeniably, had an indelible effect on their national character, so to speak. The myth of the Middle West as the symbol of American pastoralism and the center of American urban industry influenced how blacks who came from the South saw the country and themselves. As James Shortridge suggests in his *The Middle West: Its Meaning in American Culture,* ". . . the Middle West is defined essentially by its relationship to the West." In effect, coming to the Middle West meant that blacks confronted the mythology of frontier, wilderness, and urban design, the various cultural ways that Americans go about the business of thinking about nature and spaces, in a much different formulation than in the South. (The Middle West came into vogue as a significant regional term in 1912, just as its myth as an American place was being fully and triumphantly articulated, a mere few years before the beginning of the great black migration from the South. So, we have an interesting conjunction of a place defining itself at the same historical moment as a people are beginning to redefine themselves.) In his autobiography, *Miles,* Miles Davis made much of his Illinois roots when he compared his outlook to that of fellow jazz trumpeters Dizzy Gillespie and Louis Armstrong: ". . . I'm from the Midwest, while both of them are from the South. So we look at white people a little differently." He elaborated when speaking of saxophonists Charlie Parker and Coleman Hawkins: "We—Bird, me and Bean—were all from the Midwest. I think that had a lot to do with us hitting it off musically and sometimes—at least with Bird—socially; we kind of thought and saw things alike."

Ralph Ellison explains the significance of his midwestern background in the introduction to his collection of essays, *Shadow and Act* (1964):

> Anything and everything was to be found in the chaos of Oklahoma; thus the concept of the Renaissance Man has lurked long within the shadow of my past, and I shared it with at least a half dozen of my Negro friends. . . .
>
> One thing is certain, ours was a chaotic community, still characterized by frontier attitudes and by that strange mixture of the naïve and sophisticated, the benign and malignant, which makes the American past so puzzling and its present so confusing; that mixture which often affords the minds of the young who grow up in the far provinces such wide and unstructured latitude, and which encourages the individual's imagination—up to the moment "reality" closes in upon him—to range widely and, sometimes, even to soar.

What Ellison suggests here and throughout *Shadow and Act* when he discusses his Midwest is that it was in "the territory" that African-Americans, perhaps for the first time, certainly with more intensity than they had had before, learned something about living in a democratic culture, limited though it may have been, which led to the fantastically humane and harshly disciplined development of their music. They learned how to feel truly what they were instead of how they should feel or pretend to feel for whites. It was as if life in the slave quarters had finally been given space to expand and air to breathe.

Midwestern Swing

One of the best black swing bands—one of the best swing bands, period—was based at Detroit's Greystone Ballroom from 1926 through 1941, although its glory years were roughly from 1928 to 1934. The Greystone was probably "owned" by the Jewish-dominated Purple Gang, which controlled graft and bootleg booze in Prohibition-era Detroit, a key city in smuggling foreign liquor because of its proximity to the Canadian border. And the new hot black music called jazz, as the early careers of Cab Calloway, Duke Ellington, and Earl Hines can attest, became the central feature of the ambience of gangster-controlled nightclubs, to the patrons entertained and drinking. Led by circus drummer William

McKinney and star trumpeter and arranger John Nesbitt, McKinney's Cotton Pickers (Jean Goldkette's booking agency gave the band its condescending name) became a particularly redoubtable band when the famed Don Redman became musical director in 1927, leaving Fletcher Henderson for whom he had written scores from 1923 to 1926. The band had the propulsive drive of, say, Count Basie or Jay McShann and immaculate ensemble playing of, say, Jimmy Lunceford or Fletcher Henderson. Along with the Savoy Sultans of Swing, McKinney's Cotton Pickers were probably the best unsung swing band in jazz. They built their reputation almost entirely in the Midwest.

It is one of the least recognized facts of American popular culture that the Middle West—an area that runs from, say, Cincinnati to Kansas City, from Detroit to Oklahoma City, from Chicago to St. Louis, from Alton, Illinois, to Little Rock, Arkansas—is responsible for most black popular music in America. From Scott Joplin to Miles Davis, from Charlie Parker to Jimmy Rushing, from Curtis Mayfield to Sam Cooke, from Jimmy Blanton to Donny Hathaway, from the Isley Brothers to Brother Joe May, the Gospel Thunderbolt of the Midwest, this area was pivotal in the development of virtually every style of black music. The Middle West is where jazz came in the 1920s when King Oliver and Louis Armstrong migrated to Chicago. It is where blues became a formalized 12-bar musical pattern at the turn of the century, in places like St. Louis and Evanston, and where it became electric with the coming of the great post–World War II bluesmen like Muddy Waters, Howling Wolf, Buddy Guy, Elmore James, B. B. King, and Little Walter. It is where jazz redeveloped and redefined itself as swing in Kansas City in the 1930s and it is where Charlie Parker emerged from the Jay McShann band to reshape jazz as bebop in the 1940s. Illinois native Miles Davis made jazz cool in the 1950s, and Missourian Chuck Berry reinvented Rhythm and Blues as a youth music that a white deejay from Cleveland, Alan Freed, was to call Rock and Roll. From Coleman Hawkins to Screamin' Jay Hawkins, from Joe Turner to Tina Turner, from Milt Jackson to Michael Jackson, from Roland Kirk to Bobby Watson, the Middle West has been a central, even mythological, location for black popular culture and black popular music. And the three principal musical cities in this area have been Detroit, Chicago, and Kansas City.

From Detroit alone, after World War II, came such talents as Yusef Lateef, Thad, Hank, and Elvin Jones, Della Reese, Little Willie John, Tommy Flanagan, Kenny Burrell, Jackie Wilson, Barry Harris, Donald Byrd, Aretha Franklin, Paul Chambers, Roland Hanna, Alice Coltrane, and Charles McPherson, as well as, of course, the talent that came out of Motown after 1959. Why did Detroit become such a hothouse of musical talent after the war? It is difficult to pinpoint a precise answer but part of it lies in the intense emphasis on musical education among Detroit blacks. It is a common myth that blacks learn about music in their churches and like all myths it has a considerable amount of truth. Yet black secular music education provides as much, if not more, training for blacks who seek a music career than churches do. For instance, Ralph Ellison, in writing about jazz guitarist Charlie Christian, describes music education in the black Oklahoma school he attended: ". . . harmony was taught from the ninth through the twelfth grades; there was an extensive and compulsory music-appreciation program, and . . . a concert band and orchestra and several vocal organizations."

At the turn of the century, E. Azalia Hackley, a light-skinned black woman from Detroit who was trained as a soprano, adopted the musical education of black youth as her mission; she was called "Our National Voice Teacher" in the black press and was wont to stop for 15 minutes during her recitals and give her audiences lessons in musical appreciation and voice training. From Hackley's instructorship to that of such storied black Detroit public-school music teachers as Ernest Rodgers, Orville Lawrence, and James Tatum, Detroit black youth have been reared in a vibrant musical atmosphere in their public schools. The annual E. Azalia Hackley Program featuring black composers and black classical performers started in 1943, and such noted black Detroit performers as Rogie Clark, Robert A. Harris, and Charles Coleman (also music critic for Detroit's black newspaper, the *Michigan Chronicle*) have been featured in various years. Indeed, an aspect of black music education that is not as written about as it should be is how much blacks, in their schools, are exposed to classical European music, marching-band music, and pseudo-classical show tunes, and how much these forms of music have been traditionally enjoyed in the black community and not necessarily by the black bourgeoisie only. Blacks have often found some of these forms as attractive, as much a part of their cultural language—as they rightly should—as the musical forms that are more expressive of their own African-derived aesthetics and sensibilities, and this has influenced overall the shaping of their popular music.

Consider this fact about Motown: The three major early groups of the company—the Supremes, the Temptations, and the Miracles—were put together and rehearsed at their high schools. They were not church groups; in fact, the members did not attend the same church, and in various autobiographies there is little talk about the influence of the black church in their music. For instance, Smokey Robinson speaks about the influence of Sarah Vaughn, and Mary Wilson singles out the McGuire sisters, Doris Day, and Patti Page as her personal favorites when she was growing up (an indication, among other things, that the popular-culture broadcasting devices—radio and television—not only exposed white audiences to black music but, just as important, exposed black audiences to white music, and that black musical taste could be just as pedestrian as the white mainstream or that white mainstream tastes ought not to be routinely stereotyped and dismissed more so than black tastes are subject to be). Black music has been equally a product of secular and sacred forces and impulses. One finds this is true equally of Ray Charles, who became closely tied with the secularization of black gospel although he never learned his craft in a black church but rather at the school for the blind he attended and on gigs, and of Michael Jackson who, true to his Motown roots, also put a great deal of gospel fervor into his music but who had "music class and band in the Gary [Indiana] schools" where he grew up.

Here are two undeniable facts: First, Motown could not have happened without a strong public-school music-education program in Detroit, even if many of its performers were musically illiterate. The session musicians, the arrangers, and often the producers were not, and nearly all of them were trained in the public schools of Detroit. Moreover, the performers themselves received some musical training and exposure to music in school, which in many instances turned out to be highly influential. Second, Motown could not have happened anywhere else but in the Middle West, despite the fact that the greatest number of R and B independent labels were located in Los Angeles. (This is not where the greatest number of black artists originated or honed their craft, and as blacks were mostly shut out of both the movie industry and Las Vegas during the Cold War period of 1945 through 1960, Los Angeles was not an especially supportive environment in many respects.) For it was in the Middle West, finally, until 1970, despite New York doo-wop and the Brill Building, Philadelphia with the Twist, the Italian teen idols, and Kenny Gamble's record store at 15th and South Streets, or the proliferation of record labels in Los Angeles and a bopping Central Avenue down South Central Way, where the creative crucible of black music existed.

Crossing Over

But Motown would not have succeeded without a crossover rise in the interest in black music, particularly in postwar Rhythm and Blues. Several factors conjoined to make this possible: First, after the war, big bands and swing were passé, particularly because big bands were no longer economically feasible. Ellington and Basie, veritable institutions and the most important big bands in American music history, continued to produce new and exciting music, but most black bands disappeared, and those white swing bands that continued, with the exceptions of Stan Kenton, Buddy Rich, and Woody Herman, became, in effect, fossilized "oldie" acts.

Second, the invention and growing popularity of the electric bass changed entirely how popular music was conceived; contemporary popular dance music eventually was built around the sonic phenomenon of the electric bass. Electric instruments generally tended to find their first practitioners among black musicians because they were usually regarded in white mainstream circles as being freakish, novelty items. After blacks have created a system of playing these instruments the better to reinvent their own music, white musicians will then begin to use them extensively and create further innovations.

Third, the popularity of white covers of black Rhythm and Blues in the 1950s conferred a kind of respectability and mystique on the black versions, which led many white teenagers to seek out the real thing in curiosity and in quest of hipness (as was shown in Alan Freed's *Mister Rock and Roll,* for instance). These same white teenagers helped fuel the entire youth culture movement and many of them wound up figuring in the civil rights movement, in part because of their exposure to this music. Teens, with more expendable money, became a real presence in the mass marketplace in the 1950s. What made Motown possible was not that Elvis Presley covered R and B but that Fats Domino, in the end a more significant artist, not only crossed over with R and B hits in 1955 but with a Country and Western tune, "Blueberry Hill."

What was indeed far more radical than the Presley success in the mid- and late-1950s was the prominence of three black male romantic balladeers and show-tune singers—Johnny Mathis, Nat King Cole, and Sammy Davis, Jr., by the end of the decade. Davis made it big in the 1956 Broadway show *Mr. Wonderful,* which was specifically written for him by Jule Styne. Cole, enjoying many years of crossover success since 1948 with "Nature

Boy" and "Mona Lisa," had a short-lived television variety show in 1956 (although the show was unable to find a single national sponsor). By then he had become one of the most successful ballad singers in American popular-music history. Mathis broke big with "Wonderful, Wonderful," in 1958, made an album of standard romantic ballads in 1959 entitled *Open Fire, Two Guitars,* and became not simply a successful singer but, with youthful good looks and slick hair making him appear, to white and black taste, a bit exotic like an Indian, he was, in short order, a teenage heartthrob among both black and white girls. He appeared on his album covers more in idealized and stylized drawings and photographs than virtually any other black male artist of the period. Indeed, in *Life Magazine*'s 1958 feature on Rock and Roll, whose "most numerous fans are girls aged 8 to 16"—an article, in effect, about teen idols—Johnny Mathis is the only black singer mentioned, and with an accompanying photograph, especially surprising as Mathis's singing style was not remotely Rock and Roll.

Black male singers found it difficult to make it in romantic balladry because of the open sexual appeal needed for the music to go over with women listeners. The entire white commercial music establishment frowned upon, and felt great unease about, making a black male a legitimate sex symbol. Indeed, the fear of miscegenated sex appeal explains, in part, why such true black Rock and Roll artists as Chuck Berry, Fats Domino, or Little Richard were not promoted as were lesser white teen idols. The other factor was age, as many black male artists associated with Rock and Roll, like Berry and Domino, were considerably older than the white girls who were crazy about their records. But the success of Mathis, Cole, and Davis—which came about in part because the black male as sex symbol was making his presence felt in popular culture in the 1950s—was an enormous breakthrough that helped ease the way for Motown artists, although the first genuine black male Rock and Roll teen idol would be Twist King Chubby Checker, who did not record for Motown. (Interestingly, Checker, in an emergency for Dick Clark's "American Bandstand" show, covered R and B performer Hank Ballard's "The Twist" for a huge crossover hit in 1960, the first time a black crossed over by covering a black R and B tune, creating a dance craze in the process. Checker's youth and manner, and his lack of reputation as an aggressively sexual R and B artist, put the song over for white mainstream audiences, including adults. Gordy had never been a fan of Ballard's more salacious material, such as the mid-1950s hits, "Work with Me, Annie" and "Annie Had a Baby," and with his unerring sense for cultural trends, starting with the comic book industry's self-imposed, self-regulatory code of 1954 to rid itself of exposed breasts and horrific violence in the name of protecting America's youth, he made sure that in crossing over, Motown's music never brought with it R and B's more debauched element of good-timing jungle bunnies in the ghetto.)

The fourth factor that made crossover possible was the breakup of the music entertainment industry, caused by the decline of big bands and of the power of the Hollywood film in the 1950s due to the growth of television. New York Tin Pan Alley composers no longer reigned supreme. The major record labels—Columbia, RCA Victor, and Decca (soon to be MCA)—were being challenged by trend-setting small independent labels. Most R and B was recorded for small independent labels, as was a good deal of early Rock and Roll, bebop and soul jazz. Specialty in Los Angeles, King/Federal in Cincinnati, National and Atlantic Records, both in New York, Sun Records in Memphis, Apollo Records in New York, Chess Records in Chicago, Modern Records and Imperial Records in Los Angeles, and Savoy Records of Newark, New Jersey, are just a few of the companies that proliferated like mushrooms in the dark seeking local black music after World War II. As Arnold Shaw pointed out near the end of his book, *The Rocking 50s,* a comparison of the top pop songs of 1939 and 1959 found that in 1939, the Top Ten pop discs were made by only three companies—all located in New York—whereas in 1959, 39 companies produced Top Ten records and these were located in ten states. Popular music in America was truly becoming regionalized and more open. Moreover, the music that was most likely to attract adventuresome kids, the music that the majors had white artists covering, was the music of the small independent label.

By the time Gordy started Motown in 1959, he was

not thinking, as many indies owners were, that having a white cover of their own R and B was the ultimate mark of success. Gordy was thinking not only that the Motown publishing catalogue would be covered—which it has been much to Gordy's fabulous enrichment—but that Motown recordings would stand up as pop hits on their own, without benefit of covers, which has turned out to be true as well. This is how Motown changed American culture: by Gordy's insistence that *his* performers be able to sell the company's songs to whites and that *his* performers be able to play at the better-playing white venues. Gordy's objective always was to reconfigure what was meant by pop music, to reiterate in his approach that pop was as black as it was white. In this regard, perhaps the most remarkable album the Supremes made was the 1967 issue *The Supremes Sing Holland, Dozier, Holland,* wherein the group sang the songs of their producers, who happened to be, at that time, the hottest songwriting team in America. A black pop group legitimated the music of a black pop writing team and HDH's songs legitimated the Supremes. Nothing quite like this had ever happened in American popular culture before. (Ella Fitzgerald's 1957 *Duke Ellington Songbook* comes close.) And to emphasize the point, four months later Motown released the next Supremes album: *The Supremes Sing Rodgers and Hart.* They had been authenticated as a significant interpretative and stylistic group of singers, and HDH was on par with the great songwriters of Tin Pan Alley and the American musical theater.

Regarding Gordy's vision of reshaping and exploding the racial underpinnings of pop music, he took advantage of his time and place: From the early 1960s fascination with folk music, to the mid- and late-1960s quest to acknowledge the sources of popular music in urban electric blues and early forms of 1950s doo-wop, R and B, and rockabilly, there was a search for authentication and authenticity in pop music despite (or perhaps because of) its contrivance and its falsity—the sheer artistic and emotional vacuity of much of it. This "authenticity" is a service that blacks have learned to provide for American popular culture, though what was really being authenticated was the separation of black music as "race records," which was largely a political act to keep black music (and black artistic expression, generally) understood popularly as a marginal phenomenon. Motown changed this with its huge success, moving black music, largely on its own terms, within the popular-music mainstream, negotiating, with considerable aplomb, the enterprise of authenticating itself as youth music, while acknowledging, even celebrating, the R and B sources of African-American music, reaffirming, in an astonishing cultural wave, the innovative power of R and B as a pop music. The deep complexity of the quest for authentication in popular music lies in the extraordinary happenstance that all cultural innovations are subject to cooptation by a mainstream that tends to "normalize" or nonspecialize the innovations for mass consumption. These societal instances of reenforcing marginality while thwarting it by erasing its existence as a threat produces, ultimately, in differing ways, among both the elites and the masses, an urge for more authentication and innovation. This is the elementary dynamic of creation in a capitalist culture. Within a little more than a decade, from 1945 to 1959, from, say, Louis Jordan to Ray Charles, the first wash of "authentic" black music, R and B, began beneath bourgeois moral (this is dirty music), political (this music promotes race mixing and disturbs the status quo) and commercial pressures (this independent music is undercutting the power of the major record companies) to experience its own dilution and decadence, moving from a marginalized but artistically rigorous avant-gardism into an orthodoxy of mediocrity. That, as much as anything, made possible the success of Motown (and to a lesser degree its rivals Atlantic and Stax) in the 1960s era of renewed authentication, and the quest for authentication was made all the more vigorous because black people—with a revitalized political consciousness and momentous political agenda that for the first time in American history had a huge impact on the culture at large—desired it so very much.

In the 1960s the only other force in black American popular music that rivaled Motown as an authenticator was James Brown, the Godfather of Soul himself. As Bruce Tucker, coauthor of Brown's autobiography, points out, Brown was not a product of Stax, Atlantic, or Motown, but a sort of freelance presence in black music in the 1960s; and after 1965, when he became a pioneer in funk—or a kind of extremely rhythm-based, almost antisong, rifflike dance tune, he began to undermine Motown's "crossover" influence through new groups like Sly and the Family Stone and through his influence on a wide variety of established black artists, including Miles Davis, Jimi Hendrix (during his Band of Gypsies phase), Herbie Hancock, and Motown's own producer Norman Whitfield, who all began to formulate tunes in the studio based on musicians playing counterriffs on an improvised bass riff. In other words, in the late 1960s, and certainly by the early 1970s, during the height of the black power and black pride movement, many younger blacks thought Motown sounded too "white," too crossover, and not authentically "black" enough, but this was not actually a realization that grew from Motown's "sound" as much as from its marketing success and the growing tendency for young whites to co-opt Motown as their own cultural authentication. Young blacks felt simply that this music "cannot authenticate them and us, too and still be our music," as one black collegian told me back in 1972. Interestingly, Hendrix, Davis (in his electric phase from 1970 to 1975), and Sly Stone—mentioned above as three artists influenced by the funk innovations of Brown—were also influenced by the pop crossover innovation of Motown, and each had a large crossover audience. And each, in his distinct way, became entangled in the limitations of both funk and crossover, in ways that both Brown and Motown avoided, becoming in the end hideously costumed minstrels unable to escape the cultural entrapment of black "rhythm" as a stigma of stereotyped black male sexuality and clownish showmanship that became an artistic cul-de-sac. (Black life and music in America has been sullied by its two most striking characteristics: rhythm and fervor, two musical and psychic features that whites have convinced themselves that they intrinsically lack, so much the better that they might have a neurotic need for the Negroes in their midst who supply them in abundance! Motown and Brown built their music on both rhythm and fervor, but Motown managed to transcend them so that both became in Gordy's vision assertions of Negro soul and adumbrations of the American pulse of creative "force," while Brown monopolized them as blatant individual expressions of American entrepreneurial energy and drive. For both Motown and Brown, rhythm and fervor became new versions of multiplicity, of the dynamo.) That all three men—Davis, Hendrix, and Stone—in different ways, despite their remarkable success commercially and artistically, were destroyed by drugs by the mid-1970s was not surprising, even, in some ways, predictable.

Gordy could imagine that his own R and B indie would become a pop force because of the success of black-owned Vee Jay Records, located in Chicago. (There had been other black-owned record companies including, for instance, W. C. Handy's Black Swan Records, started in 1921, and Excelsior Records, launched in either the early 1930s or early 1940s, depending on one's source, by Leon and Otis Rene from Louisiana.) Started in Gary, Indiana, in 1953 by Vivian Carter and James C. Bracken, along with Vivian's brother Clarence who became the company's top A and R man, Vee Jay grew to be one of the most successful indies and one of the most successful black businesses in American history. "The company had a phenomenal track record," said Randy Wood, who became president of the company in 1963, "usually producing a hit with an artist's first or second release." The company started by recording black gospel because such acts were cheap and plentiful around Chicago but soon expanded. Among the artists Vee Jay had in its stable by 1961 were Jimmy Reed ("Ain't That Loving You, Baby," "Honest I Do," "Baby, What You Want Me to Do"), Dee Clark ("Raindrops," "Hey, Little Girl"), Jerry Butler and the Impressions ("For Your Precious Love"), the Dells ("Oh, What a Nite"), the Spaniels ("Goodnight, Sweetheart, Good-night"), and the El Dorados ("At My Front Door"). They were to have eventually the Four Seasons ("Sherry," "Walk Like a Man," "Big Girls Don't Cry"), Betty Everett ("It's in His Kiss or The Shoop Shoop Song"), the Beatles ("Do You Want To Know a Secret?" "Please Please Me," "From Me to You," "Love Me Do," "Twist and Shout"), and Gene Chandler ("Duke of Earl," "Rainbow"). Vee Jay also had a number of successful jazz acts in their catalogue, including several sidemen from Miles Davis's mid-1950s quintet: Wynton Kelly, Paul Chambers, Philly Joe Jones, and

Cannonball Adderley, as well as Wayne Shorter, who would join Davis's band in the 1960s, and Lee Morgan. Indeed, the company was generally more successful at promoting white acts and pushing non–R and B and non–pop material than Motown—most of whose excursions into something non–R and B or non-pop, such as the Melody label (Country and Western), Black Forum (spoken word, political activist), Rare Earth (white rock), and Workshop Jazz, were all aborted without sustained success. But Vee Jay also understood well its black R and B audience and their spending and listening habits. "The ghetto communities—black, Mexican, and Puerto Rican (and Mexicans and Puerto Ricans are heavy into black music as well)," Randy Wood notes, "spend proportionately more money on records than do whites. One cat will call up a friend, 'I've got the new Aretha album,' and the other will say, 'I've got Issac Hayes,' and suddenly they get a party together that way. Black music is really an integral part of the way blacks live."

Nonetheless, by 1966 when Motown was attaining the height of its glory, Vee Jay Records was going bankrupt, largely through management shake-ups and intense internal bickering between its black and white executives and among the blacks themselves. (One reason that Gordy exercised such strong control over Motown, always approving all of its product and never placing the company's stock on the market for public sale when he hit the big time, was probably to prevent internecine conflicts that could have destroyed the company.) Ewart

Abner, Vee Jay's top executive whose departure badly hurt the company, was, it is said, like Berry Gordy for whom he would eventually wind up working, an inveterate gambler as well as notorious for keeping accounts in his head. (Abner was incredibly knowledgeable about black popular music and how it is put together in a recording studio and was a considerable asset to Motown). Gordy, then, and possibly still, a gambler, was known for having lost considerable sums at Las Vegas and other high-rolling tables. It was, in fact, rumors of Gordy's gambling losses that sparked the commonly held belief that Motown was taken over by organized crime in the mid-1960s. It is impossible to say whether this is true; virtually everyone connected with Motown past and present, including Gordy himself, denies it. Nelson George, in *Where Did Our Love Go?*, makes a persuasive argument against it. In any case, there is a certain capacity for huge risk-taking among some pop-record executives. As Robert Pruter writes in *Chicago Soul*, "To be an executive in an independent record company, which depends on a continued production of hit records for its month-by-month existence, is to be a naturally gambling type."

Vee Jay was also hurt, though not irreparably, by the damaging loss of its two top white acts—the Four Seasons and the Beatles—to major labels, which may have intensified the squabbling between the white and black executives about the direction of the company. But from Vee Jay Gordy learned that it was possible to run a black-owned record company that could have crossover appeal, that could get its records played on white radio stations and pushed in white record stores. Vee Jay acts such as Jimmy Reed and John Lee Hooker sold very well in white markets. This vision not to restrict himself to just a black market was largely responsible for Motown's success, in contrast to the gun-toting Don Robey who started Peacock Records—another important black-owned indie—in Houston in 1949 and built an extraordinary blues, R and B, and gospel catalogue, including Johnny Ace, Bobby Bland, the Dixie Hummingbirds, "Gatemouth" Brown, Big Mama Thornton, the Mighty Clouds of Joy, and the Caravans.

Gordy could imagine the possibility of not restricting himself to just the black market because the period in which he shaped his vision through his apprenticeship in music—the 1950s—was the age of cultural crossover for the African-American in some striking, symbolic ways: Gwendolyn Brooks was awarded the 1950 Pulitzer Prize for poetry for her collection, *Annie Allen*. Ralph Ellison won the National Book Award for his 1952 novel, *Invisible Man*. William Demby in his 1950 novel *Beetlecreek* and Richard Wright in his 1953 novel *The Outsider* both explored existentialism and modernistic despair and dread as major themes instead of social protest. James Baldwin established himself in the 1950s as the most popular black American writer of his day; his essays appeared regularly in the most respected high-brow and middle-brow magazines, and his books were beginning to appear on the best-seller lists by the mid-fifties. Between 1945 and 1956, Baldwin, Chester Himes, Zora Neale Hurston, Richard Wright, and Willard Motley were among the black writers who wrote novels that featured white characters exclusively. Sidney Poitier became a major Hollywood film star, playing dignified if pressured characters, a far distance from Stepin Fetchit, Willie Best, Louise Beavers, and Mantan Moreland in the 1930s and 1940s; he opened the decade playing a doctor trying to make it in a white hospital against accusations of incompetence in *No Way Out*, [8] played Africans three times during the fifties in *Cry, the Beloved Country* (1952), *Mark of the Hawk* (1955), and *Something of Value* (1957), and ended the decade in *Porgy and Bess* as Porgy (a role he did not want) and as Walter Lee Younger in *A Raisin in the Sun*, both stage play and film. Lorraine Hansberry's 1959 *A Raisin in the Sun*, the most famous of all black plays, posed both the African and the American, the nationalist and the assimilationist, perspectives of the black national mentality when, on the one hand, Beneatha—who adopts the natural hairstyle or Afro as it was to be called a decade later—considers marrying the Nigerian, Agasai, and when, on the other, Walter endorses his mother's decision to move to a house in a white neighborhood after he confronts the white "welcoming committee" of Mr. Lindner who wants to buy him out. In effect, the play suggests that the African-American will be saved only through his acceptance of the three strands of his history: as a proud African who had civilizations and nations (Beneatha's halting love of Agasai), as the inheritor of the patience, endurance, dignity, and love characterized by the females of his family (Lena and Ruth), and as a proud American who came from, as Walter acknowledges, generations of obscure laborers (Walter Lee and his father).

The age of the cultural crossover encompassed much more than the literary and cinematic, however; Jackie Robinson, with obvious rage and sublime restraint, integrated Major League Baseball in 1947 and won the Rookie of the Year Award, one year after the Supreme Court outlawed racially restrictive housing covenants and five years before the Supreme Court outlawed "separate but equal" public school systems. Floyd Patterson—Catholic, intensely assimilationist, Olympic champion in 1952, ambiguous about his profession, clearly a different kind of personality from Joe Louis— became the youngest heavyweight boxing champion in history when he defeated Archie Moore for the vacant title in 1956. By the 1950s, the Negro crossing over to the mainstream had become—through Jackie Robinson—an heroic national icon and—by Supreme Court decree— national public policy.

On the other hand, crossing over meant for many blacks a new kind of activism, a keen sense of nationalistic community embedded, in an ironic yet typically American way, in the idea of integration not through simple if noble endurance of degradation but through a persistent acknowledgment of claims—from court cases like *Shelley v. Kramer* in 1948, to the Brown decisions (ruling and implementation) in 1954, to marches in the street, to the resurgence of Pan-Africanism. In this respect, the 1950s was the coming of age, the maturity of the black bourgeois consciousness as an urge to change and, paradoxically, to challenge the white racist mind, and purify the American democratic vision. In short, the 1950s taught us that there could be no democratic consciousness without a realization of the black, and, further, that there could be no democratic impulse without a recognition of black consciousness as an essential mode in the national character. This is what Ellison's *Invisible Man* was all about, and although it rejected black nationalism in the form of the antique character, Ras, the book vehemently endorses the idea of community among black folk and, even more meaningfully, in depictions such as Trueblood's family, the Golden Day, and a politically active Harlem—*the recognition of the significance of what that community wants and what it is to the overall meaning and structure of American culture.* Ellison may have thought that black folk in America were unquestionably American, and not African or primitive epigones to serve either a neurotic black or white imagination, but he did not, for a second, think that being American meant being white. James Baldwin, in his collection of essays, *Notes of a Native Son,* published in 1955 and easily the most impressive of his 1950s' books, reiterates Ellison's assertions. In this series of essays, Baldwin creates critical and aesthetic space for himself by denouncing the social protest mission for the black American writer. And he rejects his father's religion and secular vision of life, and, finally, any attempt to be anything other than both American *and* black, both "a bastard of the west" and a citizen of a world that "is white no longer, and [that] will never be white again." Baldwin also articulated memorably the complexity of what ties black and white together, something that Berry Gordy could not have expressed as well but intuitively understood: "It must be remembered that the oppressed and the oppressor are bound together within the same society; they accept the same criteria, they share the same beliefs, they both alike depend on the same reality." But the maturation of this intricate consciousness created not simply a black market to be served by black businesses or a black community ennobled by its own quest for self-definition, although these two are, doubtless, important, but rather what was brought forth was a complex black public that demanded to be served and recognized by the larger society itself. The election of the Rev. Adam Clayton Powell, Jr., to Congress in 1945 and what he articulated through his rhetoric and behavior while there is very much a symbolic rendering of the black, R and B "nation," in effect, as a triptych: a market that demanded public accommodations, goods and service, and equal value and access for its dollar with the whites; a community worthy of respect for its accomplishments and acknowledgment of its aspirations; and a public that sought a reflection of its own varieties of tastes and types in the larger world.

If America entered the Cold War as the strongest, richest, and freest nation ever in human history (some would question the last, of course), blacks, despite their constrained circumstances, had to feel a certain bold expansiveness and a tempered sense of responsibility as citizens, inadvertent or not, of this republic. Jackie Robinson's response to Paul Robeson in 1949 when summoned before the House Un-American Activities Committee seems more fraught with complexities than perhaps might appear at first blush. Robeson had said that blacks would not and should not fight in a war against the Soviet Union: "We do not want to die in vain anymore on foreign battlefields for Wall Street and the greedy supporters of domestic fascism. If we must die, let it be in Mississippi or Georgia. Let it be wherever we are lynched and deprived of our rights as human beings. Let this be a final answer to the warmongers. Let them know that we will not help to enslave our brothers and sisters, and eventually ourselves." Robinson, obviously the most famous college-educated black person in America at this time, was called especially by Congress to refute what was, to many whites, a statement tantamount to treason. Part of Robinson's statement read:

> White people must realize that the more a Negro hates Communism because it opposes democracy, the more

he is going to hate any other influence that kills off democracy in this country—racial discrimination in the army, segregation on trains and buses, job discrimination because of religious beliefs.

If a Communist denounces injustice in the American courts, or police brutality, or lynching, that doesn't change the truth. . . . A lot of people try to pretend that the issue [of discrimination] is a creation of Communist imaginations. . . . But Negroes were stirred up long before there was a Communist party and they'll stay stirred up long after the party had disappeared.

The fact that Robinson and Robeson[9] had different points of view that were of national concern and were articulated and presented in the national media is, of itself, of considerable significance. Robinson wants very much to disentangle black protest from leftist causes and Marxist identification (something that both Richard Wright and Ralph Ellison—leading black intellectuals of the period who, during the 1930s, had been "fellow travelers"—would do in the next few years with their literary works), because it devalues the nature of the protest in the eyes of whites, making them think, as many did at this time, that blacks were not even capable of realizing, on their own, the degradation of their position, and that the only whites who could possibly be interested in black people's affairs, their culture, their company, would be communists (mostly Jews, who, according to white mainstream thinking, are, to a great extent, responsible for the liberalism and atheism of the modern world) and extreme left-wing whites. It was important to the assimilationist position of someone like Robinson to emphasize the reality and persistence of discrimination, but to give the lie to the idea that the races could not and have not come together in America except under a radical European political philosophy that endorses totalitarianism. Robeson, on the other hand, takes the leftist view of a "colored world" (after all, to many Europeans, Russia itself, which Robeson professed to love, was an Asiatic nation) that must throw off European and white American imperialism, fueled by capitalist greed and unbridled racism, that keeps the darker nations under foot for economic convenience and white aggrandizement, in order to achieve self-determination and, through this, a truly just world. In his view, how can the United States preach freedom and democracy to the colonized "colored" world while maintaining its own rigid racial caste system?

In this regard, the most important book by an African-American written between 1945 and 1960 was W.E.B. Du Bois's *Color and Democracy: Colonies and Peace,* published in 1945. For in this volume, Du Bois— who was to be as harassed in the 1950s as Robeson and ultimately left the United States to live in Ghana—was to articulate the theory of a "colored" global faction where "[c]olonies are the slums of the world . . . the places of greatest concentration of poverty, disease, and ignorance . . . centers of helplessness, of discouragement of initiative, of forced labor, and of legal suppression of all activities or thoughts which the master country fears or dislikes." In short, the colonies resemble African-American ghettoes. Democracy is destroyed by racism and the forces that wish to keep down the people of color in the world. Thus, "[t]he Negro problem forces the United States to abdicate its natural leadership of democracy in the world and to acquiesce in a domination of organized wealth which exceeds anything elsewhere in the world." As the "colored" world, in its fight against European and Euro-American domination, began increasingly to associate nationalism with racial consciousness, so the African-American, through the racism he experienced in the United States, began to reinvigorate his thinking about belonging to a larger black world, about blackness being transnational, of belonging to a Diaspora, if only because American racism, as Du Bois pointed out, forced him to do so:

> . . . in the Immigration and Naturalization Service of the United States Department of Justice passengers arriving on aircraft are to be labeled according to "race," and race is determined by the stock from which aliens spring and the language they speak, and to some degree nationality. But "Negroes" apparently can belong to no nation: "Cuban," for instance, refers to the Cuban people "but not Cubans who are Negroes"; "West Indians" refers to the people of the West Indies "except Cubans or Negroes"; "Spanish American" refers to people of Central and South America and of Spanish descent; but "Negro" refers to the "black

African whether from Cuba, the West Indies, North or South America, Europe or Africa," and moreover, "any alien with admixture of blood of the African (black) should be classified under this heading" ["Negro"].

It is, thus, no insignificant fact that as some members of the black elite began to reinvent, in effect, the reinvention of an "African" consciousness for black people in the 1950s—something that continues to this day, and something that black folk have been doing in this country since the 18th century—Motown, in its own middle-brow black aspirations, became the first record company to open an office in Africa. Du Bois's book sharpened and intensified the views of someone like Robeson, but they were not necessarily views that Robinson would have found absolutely incompatible with his own. Robinson, after leaving baseball at the end of the 1956 season, became a staunch advocate of black business building, conservative Republican politics, integration, and civil rights marches.

The fact that the black public was split about the exchange between Robeson and Robinson revealed that both views had adherents and held weight among African-Americans. Robinson, who specifically mentioned discrimination in the armed forces before the Congressional subcommittee because he had been acutely and intensely affected by it, knew, as undoubtedly did Robeson, the story that during the war Lena Horne had made a stop for the black USO to entertain black troops and found them Jim-Crowed, with German prisoners of war sitting in the front. Only in America could the National League's Most Valuable Player of 1949, Robinson, play in a city, New York, and not be able to eat at one of its most famous restaurants and nightclubs, the Copacabana. Only in America could we have such an effort to recognize one's merit and thwart one's humanity coexisting so easily. The Supremes, in the summer of 1965, the summer of the Watts riot, became Gordy's first act, the only all-girl group, the first R and B's group, and the first black pop act, to play the Copa, an extraordinary breakthrough in the annals of American popular culture. By 1965, the Supremes could eat there, too.[10]

In 1955, the "colored" nations of Asia and Africa, the world faction that Robeson and Du Bois spoke about, met in Bandung, Indonesia, to consider their role in a world where European colonialism was now being challenged. The conference of so-called nonaligned or Third World nations became the figure and model for African-American unity, of African-American nationalism that Malcolm X, former street hustler turned Muslim, used in one of his most famous speeches, the "Message to the Grassroots," given in November 1963 in Detroit alongside one of that city's most popular bourgeois black Christian preachers, Albert Cleage. It was Cleage who was to become the radical race-conscious counterpart to Detroit's most famous black preacher of the day, the Rev. C.L. Franklin, father of Aretha Franklin, and considered by some to be something of a rogue and an Uncle Tom, despite his undeniable brilliance in the pulpit. (Sun-Ra's "ultra" band music of the 1950s also conjured up the vision of a "colored universe.")

And in 1955 Rosa Parks refused to give up her seat to a white man on a bus in Montgomery, Alabama, just a few months after Emmet Till, a Chicago boy, was lynched in Mississippi for whistling at a white woman or asking her for a date. In both events—one an affirmation through assertion and the other a furious denial through a falsely proclaimed innocence—we have America cringing at confronting the reality that simply will not hide itself anymore: the reality of a miscegenated culture where, beneath the mask of an inhuman racial etiquette where everyone supposedly was as separated as the twin beds in the bedroom of nearly every 1950s TV sitcom, in this mannerly ill-mannered age that was to give us the completely unruly sixties, there lurked the unquenchable thirst of interracial sex, which is, finally, what the "new" popular music as (aural, oral, and visual) spectacle in the 1950s relentlessly pantomimed, a false separation that only revealed the culture's essential fusion all the more tellingly and inescapably. Motown was the most grand and most mythic version of this spectacle, this American moment of entrapment between debasement and heroism, between art and cheap commercialism, between infantilism and something suggesting a kind of disciplined liberation, between the best and the worst of both the democratic impulse and black consciousness.

In October 1962 the first Motown Revue left Detroit on a ten-week tour, with the Marvelettes, Marvin Gaye, the Supremes, the Contours, and others. The bus tour took them through the South and the Midwest during the height of the civil disobedience phase of the civil rights movement. In May 1961 the first freedom riders had left Washington D.C. on Trailways and Greyhound buses en route to New Orleans in an attempt to desegregate terminal rest rooms and eating facilities. The freedom riders were beaten, nearly killed, and jailed. The Motown Revue, with so many young blacks on board that it must have resembled a Freedom Tour to some white Southerners, was not greeted quite so harshly; but the Motown bus was shot at, and segregated facilities and uncivil treatment were common. In 1964, when Motown released Martha and the Vandellas' "Dancing in the Street," urban riots were becoming the sine qua non of black frustration. Few blacks accepted the song on its face, insisting that it was a metaphorical theme song for black unity and black revolution. To Motown and Martha Reeves, of course, it was just another dance song. But the music and the history could not fail to conjoin. So maybe it wasn't. Could anyone truly believe that *that* song could come from *that* company, sung by those young black bewigged women, at *that* moment in American history, and not mean everything that all those black folk looting stores and throwing bottles at the police—and making in their rage the unlivable place they lived in more unlivable—thought it meant? Yet the young artists knew their significance, as Mary Wilson, one of the bewigged Supremes, wrote: "Our tours made breakthroughs and helped weaken racial barriers. When it came to music, segregation didn't mean a thing in some of those towns, and if it did, black and white fans would ignore the local customs to attend the shows. To see crowds that were integrated—sometimes for the first time in a community—made me realize that Motown truly was the sound of young America."

The Shrine
and the Seer

I'd like to hear five recordings of Louis Armstrong
playing and singing "What Did I Do To Be So Black and
Blue?"—all at the same time. Sometimes now I listen to
Louis while I have my favorite dessert of vanilla ice cream
and sloe gin. I pour the red liquid over the white mound,
watching it glisten and the vapor rising as Louis bends
that military instrument into a beam of lyrical sound.

—Ralph Ellison's *Invisible Man*

The deep-rooted Scriptural image of marital union
representing God's reconciliation with his redeemed
people and with the land, the city of Jerusalem, and the
holy temple helped to justify the hotly disputed inclusion
of the Song of Songs in both the Jewish and Christian
biblical canon, by pointing the way to interpret its songs
of sexual passion and union as an allegory signifying the
love and marriage of the Lord to Israel, or of Christus to
Ecclesia, or any of a large number of alternative
relationships. . . . [T]he canonizing of Canticles, with its
candid, detailed, and erotica physicalism, opened up a
rich stock of sensuous imagery on which later writers
could draw to embellish the austerely abstract marital
symbolism of the other books of the Bible. The result of

these complex developments is the paradox that
Christianity, which under the powerful influence of
Pauline theology has been mainly ascetic in its doctrines
and attitudes, has often employed sexual union as its
central symbol for the crucial events of Biblical history,
and for several of the churchly sacraments as well.

—M.H. Abrams's *Natural Supernaturalism*

The Sound of Young America

Red, white, black, and blue(s), Ellison's figurative colors
of miscegenated America (sloe gin, vanilla ice cream,
and Louis Armstrong singing "What Did I Do To Be So
Black and Blue?") are also the figurative colors of
Hitsville, U.S.A. made intelligible through their motto,
"The Sound of Young America"—of the Motown
Museum, now located in the same two buildings on
West Grand Boulevard where it all started. The idea that
Young America, as it were—that is, the America that has
overthrown its bondage to parents and ancestors as models, its filiopietistic homage to black oppression—would
have a "sound," not a voice, is startling yet fitting. As
Jacques Barzun theorized, the public mania for music in
the 20th century is a sign of "an increasing resistance to
words." And a "sound" suggests something that is not a
voice, something beyond and before a voice and thus beyond and before words, something both pre- and post-

civilized. But also suggested by the word "sound" is the African-American slang term for a game of ritual insulting (also called "playing the dozens" but in the Philadelphia neighborhood in which I grew up was called "sounding," each insult being called a "sound"). In that respect, "The Sound of Young America" becomes something subversive and perverse, a cannily contrived insult at mainstream America, cloaked as a seemingly innocent diversion. Here is clearly sloganized the miscegenated vision: the "Sound" being black, and "Young America" being white, as Gordy may have meant it to be, or that black kids could be mainstreamed as teenagers, too. Perhaps Motown, for the first time in American history, gave black kids a mythicized puberty of normal teenage angst.

Black Radio, Black Talk

[I first encountered Berry Gordy] playing music, and I had taken a few of his records. When you do something everybody knows about it. They'd know when I break a record. When I'd go in there and break a record everybody knew that I was doing it. That's how I got to know him. Because I played his music, and made him a lot of money. . . . [My relationship with Berry Gordy] started when [Gordy] started his record company. He had a company but it was very small. He had basically Smokey Robinson. But he had some records out, and he

wanted me to introduce Stevie Wonder and all the acts.
He knew what I was doing here. So he would let me get
the entertainers here first, and if a record came out he'd
get it to me first. As a result people would listen to me,
because they knew I would always have the top records,
and I'd have the Motown Revue when it came through,
and it would have all the stars. He was a very loyal
person. . . .

—James G. Spady, *Georgie Woods: I'm Only a Man,*
biographical account of one of Philadelphia's most
influential black deejays.

Cheerio, My deario
World and cheer-o-et
Cheerio, My deario
There's a tune in the old boy yet
Pip, pip, and all that sort of rot
Tally-ho, there he goes,
I'll see you, little darling
And good morning, someone.

—sign-off of Little Lord Fauntleroy, popular black
Philadelphia deejay of the 1950s and 1960s.

But without voices, in this instance the black personality
deejays spinning the platters and their jive, Berry Gordy
would never have succeeded in seducing America with
the Motown sound. (This is a phenomenon distinct
from the white disc jockey of the post–World War period who played Rhythm and Blues on a white radio sta-
tion, in particular Alan Freed, who went on to promote
both Rhythm and Blues and Rock and Roll in a series of

stage shows and cheap but important movies such as *Mister Rock and Roll, Go, Johnny, Go,* which heavily promoted Chuck Berry, giving him a speaking part of considerable presence, and *Rock, Rock, Rock.*) Frantic Eddie Durham of WCHB in Detroit was one of the most important on-the-air pushers of Motown records in the early 1960s. Ken Bell, an important black deejay in the mid-1960s with KJLB in Detroit, says: "If it were not for the black disc jockeys, there would have been no Motown. At first, we broke the records before the white stations did. If a record is not played on the radio, nobody accepts the record. You can't even give it away, if it's not played on the radio. And the black disc jockeys helped Motown get its sound across to the white stations. The black disc jockeys were very, very instrumental and Berry knew this and treated us accordingly."

The importance of the black disc jockey in selling black music predates the coming of Motown. As Nelson George writes: "The relationship between recorded music and radio would be crucial for the evolution of rhythm & blues, since it was to be the first major American musical style to emerge through the playing of its records on the air. . . . Coinciding with the emergence of a vast number of indie labels was the growth of black radio." Gordy, naturally, would have recognized both of these trends during his period as a record-store owner. Radio helped not only to formulate and structure black taste and aesthetics but also to formalize a black market of consumers who could be delivered to sponsors, a black public of listeners who wanted to be informed about matters of importance to them or who simply wanted access to the new medium in order to feel equal to other Americans, and a black community unified by its voices (deejays) and its music, and who could see the radio as a kind of community bulletin board, advice column, and dating service. And black radio provided all those needs.

Bell goes on to discuss the importance of the "black voice" within the black community:

> We had to play the image of being somebody in the black community. We had to be clean and sharp whenever we made an appearance anywhere. A white d.j. could show up in a tee-shirt and jeans but the blacks were highly regarded people in the black community and we had an image to live up to.
>
> Personalities d.j.s are dead now. Taping and the way records are played now killed the market for the personality deejay. Nonstop, 50-minutes of music killed the personality deejay. People are interested in music and not talk. But people still like to hear the d.j.s talk. In the 1960s and the 1970s we were the rappers. People came out to see me at clubs as if I were an artist. Now we have rap music, which shows that people still need to hear talk, still need a voice.

The many men and few women who became personality deejays on black radio in the 1960s were the voices for the sound, were the voices for the social phenomenon of urban blackness.

Living in the City

Hitsville and Motown as names conjure up both the small town and the big city (Mo' Town?, as a colleague suggested) and, in some way, encapsulate the range of black urban expressiveness and black urban mythology that is the magic kingdom of the metropolis in black American consciousness or, more precisely, in black American fantasy. For, as mentioned above, blacks came to the major cities, to middle-western cities like Detroit, with great hope as European immigrants came to America. One enters Hitsville, the Motown Museum, and is struck by how small it is; it is truly nothing more than a boxlike residential home, oddly enough on a thoroughfare in Detroit where, only a few blocks removed, are the Fisher Building, the General Motors buildings, and the Henry Ford Hospital. But the smallness of Hitsville emphasizes the myth of the black family in two ways: Again, we are reminded by the intimate residential nature of the building that Motown was indeed a "family," and second, we are reminded by its smallness about the small, cramped quarters blacks lived in when they first came to cities like Detroit. And within Hitsville, we find the original recording equipment that was used to make all those hits and realize that the machine—the dynamo, to use Henry Adams's terms—was always a sign of hope and a signification of liberation for blacks, from the car and the machines that produced them, which because of labor shortages beckoned for black hands to operate them, to such machines as the camera, television, and radio which, however waywardly, spread the image of blackness across the land. As songwriter/producer Sylvia Moy said, "We all got excited about that equipment over there [at Motown] and we were able to express ourselves creatively through a lot of equipment that was in that place over there on West Grand."

It may be true, as sociologists Stuart and Elizabeth Ewen state, that "[c]onsumption is a social relationship, the dominant relationship in our society—one that makes it harder and harder for people to hold together, to create community." But Motown as a mode of both consumption and production, indeed, as a stylization—a discipline forged from art and politics—of both, probably held blacks together better than virtually anything else in the black national community, other than the demand for equal rights. That is what the words "Hitsville" and "Motown" signify, finally: a modern black urban community built on technology, on the American bourgeois principles of consumption and production, and on the Washingtonian principles of casting down one's buckets where one is. It was, for a time, an ideal and idealized union of local black organization with a national black sense of mission and destiny.

The Women at Motown

Within the walls of Hitsville one can, through the photos and clippings, the plaques and the album covers, piece together the history of the place. One is appropriately surprised to discover the number of people who have recorded something under contract to Motown: Ahmad Jamal, Sammy Davis, Jr., Tony Martin, Pat Boone, Amiri Baraka, Stanley Crouch, Langston Hughes, Clarence Major, the Last Poets, Rick James, Willie Hutch, the Isley Brothers, Jose Feliciano, Albert Finney, Lynda Carter, Grover Washington, Jr., Teena Marie, and Bonnie Pointer. George Clinton of Parliament-Funkadelic fame was once a staff songwriter for Motown, and Wallace Terry recorded portions of his book *Bloods,* about black soldiers in Vietnam, for the company. And the company continued to be a major force in the 1970s with such artists as Diana Ross, Stevie Wonder, and Marvin Gaye coming into their own and such new major acts as the Commodores (from which Lionel Richie sprang), the Jackson Five, and Thelma Houston. But the company was nowhere like the major force it was in the 1960s when, single-handedly, it staved off the twin invasions of British popular music (from the Beatles, the Rolling Stones, and other groups in Rock and Roll and from Anthony Newley in the theater). From the producer/songwriter era of Smokey Robinson and Mickey Stevenson in the early sixties to Holland, Dozier, and Holland, who wrote and produced most of the Supremes' hits in the mid-sixties to Norman Whitfield and Barrett Strong and Simpson and Ashford at the end of the sixties, Motown enjoyed an era of near dominance in American popular music.

There are, of course, the stories of such other producers and songwriters as Ivy Joe Hunter, Hank Cosby—and Sylvia Moy who rescued the career of Stevie Wonder with the tune "Uptight" when Motown was ready to drop him because his voice had changed. Moy was never given producer's credit for that tune or any other tunes she produced for Wonder at Motown. "I cried, and cried, and cried about that when they weren't going to list me as Stevie's producer," she said. "It nearly broke my heart." Motown was a man's world and no women were ever given credit for producing records. "At that time [1964, when she joined Motown], women did not produce, even though I had the talent and I was producing," Moy continued. "I went to producers' meetings. I was given assignments. I just wasn't given the label credits. I still had my royalties. At that time, women just did not produce. I guess that was just one of those things."

But women were essential to the success of Motown: Raynoma Gordy as musician, singer, publicist, and song arranger; and Maxine Powell, who gave up her own successful charm school and modeling business to tour with Motown acts between 1964 and 1970, and who taught the singers how to walk, talk, hold a microphone, and generally provide the acts with that polished, groomed, and polite presence that made it possible for them to cross over. Although all artists, black or white, need training of this sort to succeed as professional performers, it is especially important for blacks who, as James Baldwin noted, must appeal to mainstream white taste by always being mannerly and likable. (As Beatle George Harrison said on first meeting the Supremes, "We expected soulful, hip girls. We couldn't believe that three black girls from Detroit could be so square!" Whatever stereotype of the urban black street girl Harrison may have been expecting, he was not prepared for a face-to-face confrontation with a fierce black bourgeois ambition that sought to consolidate, not rebel. Martha Reeves describes a similar incident when she and her Vandellas were mistaken for "party girls" by actor Robert Mitchum.) Moreover, this training made the Motown acts more appealing to many blacks because the performers represented a middle-brow impulse to respectability without abandoning their sense of origin. There was also Loucye Gordy, whose extraordinary bookkeeping and bill-collecting abilities kept Motown fiscally sound in the early years when record distributors were slow in paying, tours were not very profitable, and cash flow was tight.

Finally, there was Diana Ross, upon whose back Motown's crossover movement was built once Mary Wells, the singer Gordy originally intended to use to pitch his crossover appeal, flew the coop on her twenty-first birthday after she had several number-one hit records. (She was never heard from again as a major hit-making singer.) Gordy intended from the beginning, to cross over with a woman because he felt that black women were less threatening and, in some ways, more comforting to the white public than a black man would be, especially with the intense sexuality and sensuality that the "new" popular music of Rhythm and Blues and Rock and Roll suggested. The fate of Diana Ross and the Supremes reveals how Gordy saw women as both necessary and expendable. The messy ouster and subsequent pathetic downfall of Florence Ballard—founder of the group and at one time its lead singer until Gordy decreed that Ross has a more sellable and commercial voice— was as inevitable as the unfolding fate in a Greek tragedy. Gordy had no choice but to get rid of one of the women in the group once Ross was made the star in order to show the public and Ross herself that the other women were expendable; the founder of the group was as good as anyone for that symbolic chore. Moreover, it was necessary for Ross's own success that not only Ballard not succeed once she left the group but that the group itself, once Ross left, not succeed. The success of the entire group, once Ross was a star, had to hinge on Ross's presence. Thus, no other woman leaving the group could succeed and the group could not succeed without Ross. (The Supremes, without Ross, had a few successful records, notably "Up the Ladder to the Roof" but quickly faded as a viable act.) In order to make one woman indispensable in the public's mind, several other talented women had to be, in effect, wasted. Not only the other women in the Supremes but the other women singers at Motown, all of whose careers faltered once the big push to make Ross a star started: Kim Weston,

Martha Reeves, the Marvelettes, Freda Payne, Gladys Knight, and Brenda Holloway, to name a few.

When Gordy financed the film *Lady Sings the Blues* (1972) as a star vehicle for Ross, he insisted on so distorting the life of the famed jazz singer Billie Holiday, upon whose autobiography the film is supposedly based, that in effect he simply swallows the life of Holiday into an ocean of pop-culture kitsch for the benefit of Ross. Put another way, what interested Gordy most about the life of Holiday as a vehicle for Ross was precisely what interested Ross herself: that Holiday was the only sufficiently gigantic black bitch-goddess of popular culture whose art could legitimate Ross's own standing as the reigning black bitch-goddess of her own day. Holiday's life, the conventions in black popular music she represented, and the entire reason for her addiction to heroin (abusive men who mistreated her; lack of proper recognition of the magnitude of her artistry) were made expendable for a film bio in the Hollywood tradition of whitewashed garbage. In this film, directed by Sidney J. Furie but orchestrated by Motown's chief executive, Gordy cleverly combined different strands of his crossover appeal element, making Holiday's stint with the white Artie Shaw band (called Reg Henley in the film) the major tour and the only recognizable swing band performance in the film—in effect, making Holiday a crossover star which, in partial truth, she was, although in a far more profound way than the film suggests—while having Ross's Holiday introduced to drugs by one of the whites in the band (bi-ographically untrue), a kind of racist sop to blacks. Ross was nominated for an Academy Award in what had to be one of the worst acting jobs of all time, a combination of gestures that resembled imitations of both Mary Pickford and an hysterical woman victimized by bad psychoanalysis (although this performance is no worse than those of some whites who have won the Oscar).

But the whitewashing of the life of Holiday also ap-pealed to blacks who want, as much as anyone, to have their fantasy lives fit the Hollywood formula of true love and family happiness. Gordy certainly wanted no part of earlier films about black male jazz artists, such as *Sweet Love, Bitter,* made in 1967, and loosely based on the life of Charlie Parker (adapted from the novel *Night Song* by John A. Williams), that starred comedian Dick Gregory, or *A Man Called Adam,* 1966, staring Sammy Davis, Jr., as a tragic, ill-tempered trumpeter (loosely based on Miles Davis as a model, I suppose, inasmuch as Cicely Tyson, who was Miles Davis's girlfriend at the time, was featured as the love interest in the film) strug-gling for his manhood and his artistic vision in a racist and philistine society. Both of these films end with the deaths of the artists; *Lady Sings the Blues* ends with Holiday triumphant at Carnegie Hall. Gordy's film is not so much about the downfall of a brilliant artist as it is about the struggle of a black woman to become a respectable lady in this society with the help of a decent, proud man (an interpretaion of Holiday that would have an especial appeal to blacks with middle-brow impulse). Gordy may have been interested in making Ross a "black Barbra Streisand" but he was just as interested in making both Ross and her male lead, Billy Dee Williams, black versions of, say, Clark Gable and Doris Day. In effect, Gordy was interested in creating, for the black public, black stars who transcend the immediate film that the audience may be watching.

He succeeded much better, a year later, with *Mahogany,* which he directed and financed, although the film was not as well received critically and did not do so well at the box office. *Mahogany* is a brilliant film, mythifying, in concise symbolic terms, the middle-brow black struggle for identity. Ross, whose acting is much better here because the role is much closer to her own experience, plays a ghetto-dwelling, struggling, department-store clerk who wishes to be a high-fashion designer. She is accidentally discovered by a famous fashion photographer, played by Anthony Perkins, who makes her into a successful model. In the meanwhile, she is torn between her love for Billy Dee Williams's character, a committed activist in the ghetto running for public office, and her love of success and the artsy European life to which she has grown accustomed. Gordy here has superbly conflated the old Hollywood formula of a woman torn between her career and her man with the identity struggle of the successful middle-class black (Have I left my people? Have I sold out? Do I truly prefer white to black?). There is the usual homophobic distress here in the confrontation between Perkins, whose character is gay, and Williams, whose manhood is never questioned, much to the pleasure of his black audience, as well as the usual conflation of homosexuality, pointless existence, brutal capitalism, inhuman artifice, captive sexuality, and bigotry that characterize Europe and white life, generally, as a kind of velvet chamber of horrors and oddities. Mahogany ultimately returns to the ghetto to help her man, and, thus, returns to her blackness and her people. The film does more to mythify Ross herself as dramatizing the dilemma of crossover success than it does anything else. (Toni Morrison used the same dilemma to good effect in her 1981 novel *Tarbaby*, whose Jadine character is an obvious reworking of both Mahogany and Ross.) In the scenes in the Chicago ghetto, the film does not dramatize poverty or the profundity of that experience as much as it simply does what Williams's character accuses Perkins's character of doing: photographing it for aesthetic contrast and effect. But, naturally, Gordy is not interested in the poor. He is interested in dramatizing only the blacks who wish to succeed, even those who wish to succeed by helping the poor. Gordy proved himself to be an adequate director—competent, in fact—although the film has at times the feeling of a record being slapped together or mixed down. However, he never directed another.

The Shrine

Gordy moved Motown to California in 1970 (it became official in 1972), a move he felt was necessitated by the company's overwhelming success in the 1960s and the importance of expanding in the same lucrative arenas of mass entertainment—original Broadway cast albums, Hollywood films and soundtrack albums, television production—as the major labels in the music business, all of whom are tied to larger mass-entertainment conglomerates. That there is bitterness in the black community because of Gordy's departure, that there is a sense of abandonment and devastation, cannot be gainsaid even today, more than thirty years later. The sense of abandonment (felt by both the local Detroit and national black communities) was exacerbated when Gordy sold Motown in 1988 to Boston Ventures for $61 million (without the Jobete music publishing catalogue). Motown was sold again in 1993 to Polygram for $301 million, a sale that included 30 artists, the most valuable of whom is Boyz II Men, and a catalogue of 30,000 master recordings. Gordy remains the chairman of the company.

Gordy left to black Detroit what was to become the museum (1987), which Michigan made an historical landmark in 1988—a combined tourist trap and institutionalized set of memories like Graceland, operating on a particularly impassioned nostalgia that the merchants of popular culture strive to induce in nearly everyone about his or her youth.

I first visited the Museum at the time of the second annual tribute to Marvin Gaye, which appears to be the museum's annual fund-raiser, entitled "What's Going On?" The tribute was held at Clubland on April 2, 1991, Gaye's birthday, but as Gaye suffered the misfortune of having been murdered by his father in 1984 on April 1, it was difficult to tell what was being commemorated. As Eliot wrote, "[W]ere we led all that way/for Birth or Death?" Smokey Robinson flew in to host a fairly inept affair. At first, the winners of an essay contest were announced; it was apparently open only to the senior class students of Cass Technical High School (a school Gaye did not attend since he grew up in Washington, D.C., not Detroit). The topic was "What's Going On . . . How Do We Make a Better Community, a Better World?" Just the sort of grandiose topic that makes a gesture toward social relevance and political awareness as it blunts the most remote possibility of producing either good writing or coherent thought. The winners were all girls which, surely, induced some in the audience to lament a favorite refrain these days: Where Have All the Young Black Men Gone? . . . Dead and Buried, Every One—so we are led to believe, and perhaps it is true. Once this portion of the show was stumbled through, it staggered into the musical performances, with various acts that ranged from amateurish to boring. The Contours, the main act and an old-time Motown group, was an intriguing finale. They performed their two major hits, "First I Look at the Purse" and "Do You Love Me (Now That I

Can Dance)?" but they also performed a kind of truncated history of 1960s soul: The Righteous Brothers' "You Lost That Loving Feeling" and two songs by Sam and Dave, "Hold On, I'm Coming" and "Soul Man," the Contours wound up subsuming two major aspects of 1960s pop music—blue-eyed soul and Issac Hayes/David Porter Stax soul—into a Motown mosaic. There was something disheartening about this compression of cultural history into a parodic medley by tired, middle-aged men.

The tribute focused mostly on Gaye's "What's Going On?"—the 1971 hit album that Gordy at first did not wish to release, thinking it to be, in the words of a true pop-music mogul, "insufficiently commercial." I am not sure if the tribute every year will be called "What's Going On?" yet there hardly seems another appropriate name for it from Gaye's music that could signify a kind of dignified social consciousness that black fund-raising events these days, as in days past, must have. Uplift must never be far from the minds of people who, in the end, either are not thinking seriously about it anyway and just using it as a way to bring black people together or are thinking of absolutely nothing else and so are constantly overwhelmed by the utter impossibility of ever bringing black people together.

"What's Going On?" is probably the greatest, most storied album that Motown ever released, far more sophisticated as a concept album than what the company previously issued, such as Christmas LPs and records like "A Bit of Liverpool" by the Supremes or "Tribute to Nat King Cole" by Gaye. In a series of striking and dramatic mood-music arias, Gaye, through admittedly banal lyrics—conveniently printed on the gatelike album cover as was the custom of the day so that songwriters might appear to be poets and albums might take on the resonance of a book—provides a black Christian vision of despair in a world of war, drug addiction, environmental abuses, and racism. (The musical antecedents of this album include Pharaoh Sanders' "Karma," John Coltrane's "A Love Supreme" and the mid-sixties protest songs of Oscar Brown, Jr. and Nina Simone.) What is most notable about this album in the Gaye *oeuvre* is its *sui generis* quality; he made no record like it before and, with the exception of some suggestion of pop political consciousness on his soundtrack LP, "Trouble Man," made no record like it after. His music, otherwise, was consumed and subsumed by sex, an image and direction that both distressed and delighted the disturbed and drug-addicted singer throughout his career. ("Baby, please don't hesitate or I may have to masturbate" are the fade-out lyrics on "Sexual Healing," his last big hit single.) Yet "What's Going On?" is a perfectly realized piece in Gaye's total vision, and the reason the album remains so beloved among blacks is that Gaye is clearly playing the role of the seer (even if his vision may have been partly drug-induced, as it is reported that he consumed "mountains of cocaine" in order to keep up his muse to complete the album). It is a jeremiad. On the cover we see a well-dressed, bearded Gaye—the first time he was shown with a beard, a cogent dismissal of his hope to become a mainstream crooner—standing in the rain, apparently on the grounds of his home. There is a swing set in the background. He has a concerned, even troubled look, the look of a prophet. Just as commentators have suggested that only through sexual metaphor can the Christian vision be made plain and intelligible to its believers, so Gaye subconsciously believed that the social vision of a miscegenated culture can only be made plain through sexual metaphor, through the yearning for union, which is what all pop sex songs are about. On the inner part of the cover of "What's Going On?" we see the social result of that union, the family, which is celebrated with a montage of scrapbooklike photos, where the Christian vision and the vision of black unity can blend—photos all the more strange because Gaye's home life as a child in his father's house and as a married man was so unhappy (he was married, at one time to Gordy's sister Anna). The album was simply a bridge from Gaye, the 1960s "fella" who posed innocently as a sexual object for women, to Gaye in the 1970s, the middle-aged sexual gaucho who fears impotency.

"Funny," Gaye once said, "but of all the acts back then [the 1960s], I thought Martha and the Vandellas came closest to really saying something. It wasn't a conscious thing, but when they sang numbers like 'Quicksand' or 'Wild One' or 'Nowhere To Run' or 'Dancing in the Street,' they captured a spirit that felt political to me. I liked that. I wondered to myself, with the world exploding around me, how am I supposed to keep singing love songs?" But like Countee Cullen, another black artist torn by his Christian and pagan (sexual) inclinations (and another black artist reared by a seemingly homosexual or transvestite black father who was a minister), Gaye the seer never was of a divided mind. He always saw the world through Christian lenses whether he was singing about sex or politics; indeed, for Gaye as a Christian and as an American black male, sex was indistinguishable from politics and from religion.

But central to Gaye's vision in "What's Going On?" is the father. The album cover depicts Gaye as father figure, as patriarch, in a sense, and in the songs he cries out to his Father (God) and to all fathers to recognize their sons. David Ritz, Gaye's biographer, is right to locate Gaye's torment in his hatred of his father (a minister who was a wife beater and a child abuser, according to Ritz), whose love Gaye desired but found impossible to obtain and, in some measure, repulsive to contemplate. Gaye sought other father figures in his career: Harvey Fuqua of the Moonglows, his first professional secular group, "Pops" Gordy, who once stopped Gaye from committing suicide, and Berry Gordy himself, who never completely understood his moody but most prized male singer. But Gaye was never reconciled to his real father. There remained only the intense hatred of a father who wanted his drug-addicted son dead and a son who wanted his drunken, cruel father dead: another instance of the expendability of black males through their self-hatred. They hated each other so much because they so deeply loathed themselves and what each saw of himself in the other.

The tribute survived and succeeded, such as it did, on the evocation of memory; it may be that as a political art "What's Going On?" is still vital today, but we are not sure if that is the case or if it is the memory of what had been vitality that makes it vital still. In Robert Townsend's film tribute to R and B, *The Five Heartbeats,* which was in the theaters at the time of my visit to Detroit, we have an almost unbearable, if at times, clumsy and inartistic claim made to memory and to fathers. It is about a group that seems to collapse our memories of 1950s groups—like Lee Andrews and the Hearts, the Marcels (a tribute to black processed hair?), the Flamingoes, the Ravens, and James "Shep" Sheppard and the Heartbeats themselves—with 1960s groups like the Temptations, the Four Tops, and the Stylistics; the Dells, a group popular in the 1950s, 1960s, and 1970s were technical advisors. The film opens with Robert Townsend's character remembering the history of the group, and perhaps for blacks in particular, this need for memory is more intense now than ever, when blacks feel their identity is embattled and their position as a people compromised and diminished in American culture in more insidious ways than since the days of slavery. But this film, which is more a sentimental tribute to black male bonding than about music, fails because it does not focus on the need of and for tradition to be dramatized and acted out within the black community, so, in effect, it provides black folk with memory without history, with art without some sense of that which makes it art and makes it meaningful for the persons who make it and for whom it is made. In this conflict between fathers and sons, which drives the plot of the film, the fathers or authority figures—the group's manager, the evil record-company owner, the nay-saying father of the lead singer, the disapproving minister-father of one of the background singers—are all either killed or forgotten in the end, with the exception of the minister-father who is falsely rejoined with his son without a dramatic moment for the viewer to understand how this took place. (Unlike *Sparkle,* made in 1976, and a far more wretched movie about an all-girl group, *The Five Heartbeats* in effect closes with the black church instead of opening with it. The church is not where the singers come from but it is what they go back to, a far more powerful, middle-brow message to black folk.) The guys in the group never talk about other singers they admire, other groups—especially gospel groups and sophisticated semijazz singers like the Ink Spots and the Mills Brothers who were the main source of inspiration for these doo-wop teen combos—from whom they stole riffs or ideas. Without this articulated bridge of artistic tradition in the black community, without this liaison between fathers and sons being stated explicitly, the film's family-reunion ending is worse than dishonest; it is utter and cruel deceit, pandering to an audience in the most obvious and cheap way, because the union has not been *earned,* it has only been *earnestly desired.* Like Gaye's "What's Going On?" *The Five Heartbeats* is a jeremiad that never becomes or wants to become a jeremiad but wishes its audience to believe that it is. Townsend's film never locates real memory for blacks. It captures only the barest echo of the vitality of pop cultural memory or art. Although Townsend wishes very much to have his characters transcend the very purpose that brought them together, in the end the only authenticity of this fictive family called the Five Heartbeats lies, alas, in its commercial power and charisma. Yet the film has a certain charm for the African-American mind even in its imperfections because the emotions it evokes are emotions that only blacks, not just anyone who remembers the earlier days of Rock and Roll, can feel. In this sense, it creates a certain middle-brow power because it creates a purely black nostalgia.

Townsend's fixation on fathers brings to mind the well-regarded 1964 film *Nothing But a Man,* about a young southern black man (Ivan Dixon) and his wife (Abbey Lincoln) trying to make it in the South of the early 1960s, shot in an almost documentary style by two white filmmakers, Robert Young and Michael Roemer. The films, in truth, have nothing in common except the theme of black fatherhood and, by extension, black manhood, as well as, in different ways, evoking Motown to create a sense of memory and community. In *Nothing*

But a Man, Motown music is used as the soundtrack, thus connecting Motown with what many critics and viewers, both black and white, feel to be the most politically and artistically well-wrought black film of the post–World War II era, clearly the black lower-class and middle-brow aspiration of the assertion of black manhood and the protection of the black family. That is why, I suppose, the film was rumored to be a favorite of Malcolm X who most vigorously spoke up for an assertive black manhood and protection of the black family in the early 1960s. *Nothing But a Man* is also obsessed with the redemption of the black father, as by film's end Dixon claims his son by another woman and brings him home, reunifying his precarious marriage with Abbey Lincoln. As Gloria Foster says in the film upon the death of Dixon's father, "I know he wasn't much of a father." To which Dixon cynically responds, "Who is?" If Townsend's film suggests that the black male is framed within the community of the nightclub, church, and the family (the opening, penultimate, and final shots in the film), then the earlier *Nothing But a Man* suggests that the black man is not truly framed by his community at all, but framed by both trains and cars, symbols of industry and mobility, framed either by the community that provides work on the trains or by the lack of community that the car offers as an escape. In this sense, despite the brilliance of *Nothing But a Man* and the manipulative ineptitude of *The Five Heartbeats,* the latter is the more important work. In the Townsend film, for instance, the black preacher as middle-brow conservator of blackness and compromised resistor to whites is far better understood, if less vividly depicted than the middle-class black preacher in *Nothing But a Man,* who is, Marxist style, just a sellout and an Uncle Tom. Yet *Nothing But a Man* was made during the early 1960s when black southern churches were being bombed because of their political activity or threat of political activity. In fact, more of these churches were bombed by terrorists during those years than any other American institution, sacred or secular, was ever attacked by terrorists in the history of the republic. In *Nothing But a Man* blacks can find neither true community nor solace in virtually anything. It is either struggle or escape, a vision that resembles that of the great southern and urban black writer Richard Wright, which has a compelling power but not a sense of completeness.

Perhaps Americans, black and white, are discomfited by our popular music because it seems to serve no great ends except to make money and to provide momentary diversion. Perhaps whites are discomfited because so much of our popular music, from ragtime to New Jack Swing, from jazz to hip-hop, has been called by slang terms derived from its rhythm (ragtime, swing, Rhythm and Blues, disco) or by slang terms for copulation (jazz and Rock and Roll), a fact that is discomfiting to some African-Americans as well. Perhaps blacks are discomfited because they cannot find in the African-American origins of American music a high and lofty object, an aspiration to artistic greatness and discipline that does not seem shaded by ambivalence. Perhaps we black folk sometimes do not like the entrapment of sensuality we are forced to wear as a mask for the white imagination. Yet there is in that sensuality an expression of holiness about the wonder of the union of like and unlike things. Everything is sexual, after all, and everything seeks marriage. American popular music thumbs its nose at the respectability of art while yearning for nothing but that respectability. This contradiction is the source of its strengths, and of its imbecility, its cheapness, its nonsense, its incivility, its disregard of taste. This contradiction is the source of our democratic possibilities in art.

But music has many objectives, serves many ends. And the story of American popular music is the story of American democracy at its best and its worst, a full revelation (in Ralph Ellison's words) of America's "rich diversity and its almost magical fluidity and freedom" as well as its "inequalities and brutalities." We have had over thirty-five years of *recognized* integrated national experience in this country, and in that period the success of Motown stands as the shining hour of the American black in popular culture. Visiting the Motown Museum, attending the Marvin Gaye tribute, watching the Townsend film, listening again to the records, I am struck by the extent to which the memory of Motown, and more generally of its era, may be holding American blacks together, as we are torn apart by centrifugal social and political forces that frighten us even as they may, in the long run, bless us with a newer freedom. In the dangerous business of judging American popular art, certainly, it is difficult to tell what was Armageddon and what was just a teleological passing fancy.

Appendixes

Gordy Speaks: The *Billboard* Interview

Adam White

BILLBOARD: *So many record companies over the years have tried to become "the new Motown," and so many music entrepreneurs have tried to duplicate what you built. Yet it's hard to see how anyone could do that today.*

BERRY GORDY: Whether it can be done again, I really don't know. There are a lot of great, young, talented people out there. But the business has changed so dramatically, and the whole method is totally different than our method was.

We were in a city away from the music business and needed fresh new ideas to bring out the potential in people. We developed from the ground up. In fact, when people came to me, they were not writers, they were not producers, they were not anything. They were just smart kids off the street. That was a pioneering time. It would be very hard for another company to do what we did, because it's no longer a pioneering time. Now it's an electronic age, an age of corporate conglomerates. The pay structure is not the same: for sports figures, for entertainers, for whoever else. Everything has changed. Taking all that into consideration, I would say it would be next to impossible to do what we did.

Now, I've met people that I personally think are great, young talents. Andre Harrell, for example. He came by

Originally published in *Billboard Magazine*.

here and we talked, and I found him to be extremely bright. Some of the guys out there could do it, if it were possible to do. I'm just not sure it is possible, given the times.

BB: *You call them "kids," the people who came to you in the early days, and that's literally what they were. Teenagers, in many cases.*

BG: Absolutely. They could be channeled and directed, but they couldn't do things for themselves that much. So we did it for them; we taught them how to create.

Of course, I didn't really know, myself; I was just a competent, cocky kid who felt I knew a lot more than I did. But I had struggled to get people to hear my stuff and to listen to me. When I saw these young people coming up, I knew that they were just like me. Smokey [Robinson] was like me. All they needed was a chance to express their ideas; I would listen.

BB: *Did you have any role models in the business?*

BG: I knew almost no other writers or producers by name, but I was always fascinated by those writers who told simple, clever stories in song. Producing, as we did it at Motown, evolved. I didn't go out and hire producers.

They just developed as a result of the interaction between me and them and the environment.

BB: *What was your most frustrating obstacle?*

BG: Probably trying to get money from the distributors to stay in business! They would only pay you if you had that next hit record. It was a brand-new business—we're talking about pioneering days now—and all the independent distributors were underfinanced.

So were the independent record companies, of which I was just one. We always had to fight to get our money, along with the other independent companies: VeeJay, Scepter, King, Duke/Peacock, Chess. Whoever had the hottest record coming out would get paid [by the distributors] for their last one. That's all it was. They respected a hit.

Every now and then, we had to have a clean-up record because our money was so spread out. We had a lot of hits, but a lot of bills came with the hits. We needed a huge smash to collect all that money.

BB: *I've read that you once sent Mable John to Chicago to cut a distribution deal with Ernie Leaner.*

BG: Well, that was not true. Mable was a singer, the sister of Little Willie John; she had a record [on Tamla] called "Who Wouldn't Love a Man Like That." But she never did any business dealings or anything like that. It's funny how, after 30 years, as far as Motown is concerned, there are an amazing number of [untrue] stories out there.

I do remember that Mable used to drive me around. She really wanted to have a record career, so she would take me around. She wasn't as good as her brother, but she had a nice voice and a nice record. I usually had a car myself, but I do remember her driving me.

BB: *Before forming Motown, did you ever think about moving to New York? That was the center of the music business at that time. Or did you think there was plenty of talent in Detroit?*

BG: I never thought about going to New York, but I loved the New York sound. I had been spoiled, working with [Jackie Wilson's producer] Dick Jacobs. That big sound he got, it was just too much. I wanted a New York sound real bad.

But I never thought about moving away, never thought about whether there was or wasn't talent in Detroit. I just felt everybody was talented. And at that time, I felt I could make a hit out of anybody, you know [*laughs*]. Even though I had never been a success up until that point.

BB: *Jacobs flew you into New York for the "Lonely Tear-drops" session. Did Jackie record with the band then and there?*

BG: Yes, Jackie was right there in the studio. I think they'd rehearsed the track and got all that balanced. When I heard his voice, that crystal clear voice, come booming out over that [sound system], I knew I had something. It was just [*sighs*] an incredible, incredible thrill, hearing my song being played.

BB: *It looks like you wanted your own Jackie Wilson when Motown got started, with Eddie Holland.*

BG: Absolutely, I wanted my own Jackie Wilson. Eddie was close; he was good-looking, and he had a very smooth voice. He had a thing called "Merry-Go-Round," which I thought was really good, and, of course, "Jamie."

But Eddie didn't have Jackie's fire, that quality and that performance. Jackie was a star before I even met him, and he just had a flair about him. He was a performer all the way and he knew it. He would wink on cue with the girls. He knew what he had.

I always looked for that magic later [in others]. It was very rough for the artists who worked with me after Jackie, because I was looking for that perfection. I thought Jackie, as the first guy I ever worked with, was the norm. And, of course, it was nowhere near the norm.

BB: *Did you or Eddie Holland demo your songs for Jackie?*

BG: Eddie did most of them, except for "To Be Loved." I sang that for Jackie myself. I think "Reet

Petite" was given to Jackie by Pearl Music and Roquel Davis.

BB: *Roquel (aka Billy) recalls using one of the first electric Wurlitzers when you and he wrote together. He also told me that "To Be Loved" was done in the middle of the night, in your sister Gwen's apartment.*

BG: "To Be Loved" was born on one of the worst nights of my life. I had been served that morning with divorce papers, and I went to my sister's house in tears. The words [to the song] came easy.

Billy and I were writing partners, and the reason he was at the house that night was not to write with me, but because he was Gwen's boyfriend. Billy really had nothing to do with that song, but he and I had made an agreement. There were songs that he originally had with other writers that I was going to be part of. He was part of the songs that I wrote, and so was Gwen, because they helped me.

That's the way our relationship was: He had some songs, I had some songs. Actually, "Reet Petite" was one of the songs he started. But "To Be Loved" and "Lonely Teardrops" were songs that I wrote.

BB: *That was obviously an important relationship.*

BG: Yes. Billy and I were very different. He was a very passive person, but very good with writers—and he had good connections with the Chess brothers. Billy had not had any really big hits, but he was a nice, quiet guy. He had been around, and he had some groups that we worked with. I was the aggressive writer. I was the guy who was coming with ideas and stuff.

I had made a deal for the Miracles, and we cut some tracks at Chess. Billy had his favorites, the Five Stars and some of the other people he was working with. But I saw some magic in this particular kid, Smokey. These other people, they were good, but I didn't see in them what I was looking for.

So after we stopped writing for Jackie, Billy and I sort of split up, with me taking the Miracles, him taking the Five Stars, me taking this person and him taking that person. He went into Anna Records with my sister Gwen. We stayed friends, and I eventually bought out their company after putting "Money" [sung by Barrett Strong] with them for national distribution. It was always a good, warm relationship; we were very honorable with each other.

BB: *Before "Money" was a hit, you made "Come to Me" with Marv Johnson, then placed him with United Artists Records. "You Got What It Takes" became a smash. How did this compare with your Jackie Wilson experience?*

BG: Marv was the first guy I'd worked with after Jackie. He was not Jackie, by any means, but he became a star. In fact, he was the hottest artist we had then.

Marv was very, very good, but he wasn't as easy to work with as some of the other artists. I would have to make a lot of tapes with him, then splice a lot of things together, because sometimes he had a timing problem.

As a person, Marvin made many of our other artists aware of his star status; sometimes they would complain about his arrogance. As far as Marvin and I were concerned, it was a good relationship. He treated me fine.

We did several more records with Marvin, none of which ever got the prominence of "You Got What It Takes." There were so many things I loved about him, and each one was different. But I was also busy trying to keep [other artists] solid.

BB: *One of the stories that has passed into pop music legend is about how you met Smokey in [Jackie Wilson manager] Nat Tarnopol's office in late '57, looked at his songs—and criticized every single one. Some people would have said, "I'm out of here, I can't deal with this."*

BG: Yes, but when I went through a hundred songs and rejected every one of them, Smokey was more and more enthusiastic. He loved what I was telling him. He'd say, "I can go back and fix this one, fix that one." I thought, "This guy's either got to be the dumbest person I'll ever meet or the smartest, the nicest person or the strongest." Because he was getting more energy as I was telling him, "No, this one doesn't make it, either."

BB: *Was that what you were looking for, people who wouldn't be intimidated by criticism, by being told, "You've got something, but it needs work"?*

BG: I don't know what I was looking for, because everybody was so different. When you see what you're looking for in one person, someone else would have another quality. Norman Whitfield, for instance, had a lot of fire inside of him.

BB: *Even when he was young?*

BG: No, no, when he was young, Norman was very shy. He was a friend of Brian Holland. I used to see him hanging around; he would come to the studio. Now, I didn't like people hanging around there if you weren't either working or doing something.

One day, we needed a tambourine player. I saw Norman, and I said, "Hey, you—you! Can you play tambourine?" He said, "Yes, sir, I can." So I told him, "Well, get in there, we need to keep a beat, just two and four."

He went out [into the studio], he was keeping a beat, but he was nervous and kind of missed a couple of beats. And I said, "Hey, you—you! Out, out!" I kicked him off that session. So it took him quite a while to regain his confidence.

BB: *In an interview for the liner notes of a recent Marvin Gaye reissue, Norman gives the impression that he had his stuff together early on. "You give me money," he says he told you, "and I'll give you hits."*

BG: He may have had it together, but we never noticed it. Norman remembers very well getting kicked out of that session, but he did get very strong later. That's why I gave him a lot of credit. He kept on till he finally produced a couple of hits. And he studied my stuff, he studied "Money" and that tom-tom beat. He took that and used it on a lot of records.

Norman was probably the most underrated producer that we had. He would take the Temptations, five voices, and he would take each voice: write a song, work out a song, produce with everyone in the group doing stuff that was just phenomenal.

But Norman was very . . . [*pauses*] . . . dictatorial. He did everything that he thought I'd done to him. He said, "If you were successful [that way], then I've got to let these guys know what they're getting. I'm going to give them smashes, but they've got to work!"

I've always felt Norman worked his way up from the bottom, because my favorites were Holland/Dozier/Holland when they were hot. Once Holland/Dozier/Holland took over from Smokey, those cats were [*laughs*] phenomenal! Everything they did, whether I liked it or not, I didn't even have to hear. When they'd come into the [weekly product evaluation] meeting, it was in the pocket.

So while my focus was on them and on Smokey, Norman was out there trying to get my attention. Finally, he got it. Then as he got stronger, he voiced more of his opinions, and he won his arguments with me.

BB: *Did you get into fights over rejecting records in those Friday meetings?*

BG: Not so much fights, because I had the final say-so. But there were some very intense arguments, intense disagreements. People had the freedom to discuss and say whatever they wanted, and fight as long as they wanted to. And if they had a better argument than mine, they would win.

Logic was always the boss. I made that plain to everybody. It was not me, not them, it was not some other power, but logic. But they had to prove it or show it.

BB: *If the strongest Motowners could handle rejection early on because you were their support system, what happened as you got more involved in the business side? Did they resent your unavailability?*

BG: "Rejection" may be a slight exaggeration, because most of the records that didn't make it were because of votes at the meeting. That was rejection in a sense, but it was rejection by the peers of people who were doing it. And sometimes by themselves.

When they heard records in an open forum, they could see imperfections and a lot of things they couldn't see by listening to [a record] by themselves. That's as far as the meetings were concerned.

Now as far as my being less and less accessible, that was a definite problem. I don't think they resented it so much because of my business activities. There were always people in charge to handle them and their wishes: Mickey Stevenson, who was a strong A&R department director, and the artist-development people, the artist-management people.

I think that more resentment came as I fell more and more in love with Diana and was on the road with the Supremes. Or as I started spending more and more time with them because I saw the Supremes as the vehicle to lead Motown into a whole new world of music, and appreciation of our music.

I saw them as leaders of that movement, number one. Number two, I was falling more and more in love with Diana, and, of course, she inspired me to the hilt. And I'm sure that was resented by some of the other artists. But at the same time, I knew that it was breaking ground for the whole Motown stable. And it did.

BB: *One of the vital elements of Motown was your house band, the Funk Brothers. Some of them were experienced jazz musicians. Was it tough to get those guys to play pop music? After all, [drummer] Benny Benjamin and [bassist] James Jamerson had played with Dizzy Gillespie and other top jazz names.*

BG: Absolutely, it was hard holding them down. They constantly wanted to jump off into something jazzy or way out there. But it made the music a lot more interesting, because they would push me to the limit. Jamerson and I had major, major fights many times; he was the toughest one.

BB: *Was that because Jamerson felt he knew more than you, or because he pushed for the fun of pushing?*

BG: He felt he knew more, he felt he was better—and he was better. Jamerson had his own ideas, but we had this great relationship, and because he knew that if he did something great, I would like it even though I told him not to do it.

I would say, "Hey, you can't do that, this is not a jazz session, man. We want to stay in the groove. We want to do some good things, we want the feeling to be there and all that, but this is not a jazz session."

I didn't want to put tags on the music, because it was a mixture of a lot of stuff: gospel, jazz, blues, country and western, whatever. It was Motown music, so it was individual feelings, the band and the mix. We didn't care what it was called. As long as it was a hit.

BB: *And Benny?*

BG: Benny was into his own world, he had so many rhythms at the same time, but he kept that foot locked and everything. Jamerson was the same. They were very locked into the thing together, and they were great. Every now and then, Benny would do some crazy stuff, but he'd come right back on it. And he would look at me, smile and say something.

Jamerson and Benny would have this little competition as to who could do more and get away with it. The other musicians were more conservative, but they were just as great in their own way: Earl Van Dyke, Beans Bowles, Robert White, Joe Messina, Uriel Jones and all these guys. They were all talented and they all had their own thing.

My favorites just happened to be Benny and Jamerson. Like any artists, you have favorite people who you know can deliver the things that you want them to deliver.

BB: *One theory about why those musicians didn't receive credit on Motown album jackets in the '60s was that you were afraid they'd be poached by other record companies.*

BG: That was never a thought. We were busy making music, period. A lot of these things about credits and so forth, whatever our art department did, there was never any thought of keeping names off a record. That's crazy. That never even came up.

BB: *Some of the musicians were moonlighting, playing on sessions for Golden World Records in Detroit and other labels.*

BG: Yes, it did bother me, especially when I heard the sound coming out similar to ours.

BB. *What about pressure on Motown artists to leave for other labels? You had to deal with that almost from the start, didn't you?*

BG: The artists were being approached all the time by different people, but those approaches fell on totally deaf ears for many years. I remember Smokey coming to me once after a few hits with the Miracles. He said that a lady came to him from Scepter Records and offered him a million dollars to come with them.

BB: *I guess that was [Scepter president] Florence Greenberg. How did Smokey respond?*

BG: Smokey was insulted. He said, "How could she think I would [leave], what did she think of me?" I told Smokey, "You'll have a lot of that."

Other times, artists might mention various situations where they were approached in subtle ways, but there was never a problem until about 1964. Then Mary Wells left.

BB: *Part of the Motown magic was your hit ratio, especially compared to other labels in the industry. You put out fewer releases than most of your competitors.*

BG: Well, it wasn't done consciously. We did it because we were looking for great records—and great records didn't come that easily [*laughs*]. It was just that few records could make it through that Friday meeting. A whole lot of records stayed on the shelf.

Every record, we felt, had to go Top 10. We'd always say, "No album cuts." People [in the meeting] would say, "That's an album cut, let it go." I said, "No, no, every cut has to be something meaningful. A side and B side."

So when a record didn't make it on the A side, like Stevie Wonder's "I Don't Know Why," they turned it over and "My Cherie Amour" became one of the standards of all time.

[*Starts to sing* "I Don't Know Why"] You know, we worked so hard on that record in the studio with Stevie, and even to this day, he remembers it. I loved that record, too. "My Cherie Amour" was just a good B side.

BB: *You picked up that emphasis on quality control from working at the Lincoln-Mercury plant in Detroit?*

BG: Yes, I thought it could apply to my operation. Except that I was dealing with human beings, which made it a lot more interesting, because each one had different dreams, desires, attitudes. We let them be individuals. Each one was uniquely different, and that's why you didn't get Marvin Gaye sounding like Stevie Wonder, or Stevie sounding like Diana Ross. That only comes out of freedom of expression.

But freedom within limitations—I had some limitations. Especially with the musicians, as I've said, because they wanted to go all over the place with their jazz and stuff.

BB: *Marvin's freedom of expression seemed directed toward being Nat "King" Cole or Frank Sinatra.*

BG: He wanted to be a pop balladeer. Fred Astaire, Sinatra, that sort of thing. Top hat, cane, that was Marvin Gaye. Could he do it? Yes, Marvin was a great singer of ballads. When I signed him, it was because he had done a standard, "Mr. Sandman" [during a 1960 Christmas party at Motown]. I can still hear it today; it was great!

BB: *His very first Motown album featured standards like "My Funny Valentine," "Witchcraft" and "How High the Moon," and later on, there were his Nat Cole and Broadway albums.*

BG: Our [promotional] focus was on the Motown sound, and so because those albums didn't happen [on the charts] with Marvin, it wasn't necessarily a reflection on him. It could have been a reflection on me and the company's efforts in moving in that direction. As far as I was concerned, Marvin Gaye was a great balladeer.

BB: Of course, "What's Going On" couldn't be much further from Nat Cole or Frank Sinatra.

BG: By that time, he had fallen into another kind of mindset. He was into saving the world, so that balladeer stuff was in the background. When he was doing "Hitch Hike" and all those kinds of things, they weren't as meaningful to him. Well, "Stubborn Kind of Fellow" did mean a little bit to him, because he was a stubborn kind of fellow. But when he got into "What's Going On," his life was dedicated to awakening the minds of mankind.

BB: *Can we set the record straight on "What's Going On"? It's been said that you didn't like the record or didn't think Marvin should be singing songs like that. Is that right?*

BG: It wasn't that I didn't like the record; I didn't like the idea that Marvin, who was so popular with the women, wanted to sing protest songs. He called me when I was on vacation in the Bahamas and told me what he wanted to do. I told him, "Marvin, why do you want to talk about police brutality, the Vietnam War? You've got this great, sexy image. Why blow it?" "I don't care about no image, BG," he told me. "I just want to awaken the minds of mankind." That was heavy. I loved it when he said that. "OK, Marvin," I told him, "if you're wrong, you'll learn something—and if you're right, I'll learn something."

I learned something.

BB: *Marvin's own songs seemed to work best when someone else was involved, whether it was David Van DePitte, Ed Townsend, Leon Ware. How much did he need someone to bounce off, or someone to keep him on track?*

BG: Marvin liked to hang out with cats he liked. He could have done it by himself, perhaps, but all these people added something to Marvin. He would end up pulling it together because it was Marvin who was the genius of the group. Not only the genius—Marvin had a natural instinct for hits. He could do the national anthem and it would be a hit.

BB: *At the time, it appeared that "What's Going On" influenced Stevie Wonder in terms of the future direction of his songs and his career. How did you see it?*

BG: It's so hard to compare the two because they were so different. Marvin had a different kind of sex appeal than Stevie. Stevie was a technician; he would deal with contraptions and technology. The whole thing about Motown was individuality in all aspects.

BB: *Stevie seemed to know what he wanted once he became an adult, taking charge of his career. How rough was that for you to accept?*

BG: Stevie seemed to know what he wanted even before he became an adult. And he did indeed take charge of his career. At first, it was very rough [to accept]. Not because I didn't think Stevie could do it. He had proven that he could do things himself and that he had genius qualities and all that. What bothered me, I think, the most was the fact that he, in my opinion, was defiant.

Stevie had been at a party with me in Detroit the day before his 21st birthday, and when I got to the West Coast, there was a letter from his attorney that he was disaffirming his contracts. I was more upset about that aspect of it than I was about his being able to do it

The attorney had jumped the gun, Stevie was not going to send me a letter that day. So he fired that attorney, then he got another. After negotiating with his new attorney, Johanan Vigoda, it was agreed on.

BB: *Vigoda sounded like he was tough to deal with. Then, of course, there was the renegotiation in 1976.*

BG: Vigoda was a godsend to Stevie. He was tough, strong and brilliant, yet sensitive. He cared for Stevie like a father.

[That deal] was $13 million, it was an unprecedented thing. But even though we negotiated, we fought, Stevie never, never implied or threatened that he would leave Motown—and it turned out to be very good. He could have; he could have threatened it, but he never did.

BB: *And you know that CBS or RCA would have offered him a deal which would have . . .*

BG: . . . dwarfed ours. You understand that, and so you hope it doesn't happen. But you don't expect every artist to [turn down a more lucrative deal]. Because they would be too unhappy with themselves if they did something that they didn't really want to do.

When you work with an artist, you know that they're going to be independent. When the day comes that they decide they want to leave you—even though you expect it—that's devastating. But you do it, because a teacher has to teach.

I was driven to teach, to bring out every bit of talent and potential that a person had. You can't bring out 90% of it and say, "Well, let me hold this 10% back"—or, like you said earlier, keep their names off records. You can't even think like that.

If I had thought like that, Motown would never have been anything. You can't hold anything back, because the very nature of what we were doing was to pull out all their potential.

BB: *How much of Michael Jackson's potential was evident to you at the beginning? You obviously knew The Jackson 5 had something—and Motown turned the group into major stars—but did you expect Michael's career to turn out the way it did?*

BG: His potential was always evident. I'd always looked for the buried treasure of potential that everybody seems to have in them. Michael's treasure was never buried; it was hanging out there.

He seemed so wise beyond his years. I knew right

away he could be a big star, and I believed he could go all the way. I had no idea he could go even further than that. He did. He became the biggest star in the world.

At that very first audition, Michael sang his songs like he had experienced everything he was singing about—and he was only 9 years old. When they jumped into the Temptations' "Ain't Too Proud to Beg," Michael sang it like it was his song all along—and all of them moving together like little David Ruffins.

Michael had a knowingness about him. He paid close attention to every single thing I said. Even when my back was turned, I knew he'd be watching me like a hawk. The other kids might have been playing or doing whatever they were doing, but Michael was dead serious and he stayed that way. We connected. One of the kids finally asked me, "Mr. Gordy, does this mean you're going to sign us?" They were worried; Michael wasn't. He knew he had me.

After that, I couldn't get them out of my mind. I walked around singing [*singing*] "Oh Baby da da dee da da, da da dee da da, Oh Baby da da dee da da . . ." [*laughs*] I was creating the melody for their first song, "I Want You Back."

I brought in Deke Richards to work with me, and he brought in two other writers, Fonce Mizell and Freddie Perren. We called ourselves The Corporation. I played the melody for them, and we got to work putting the song together. We did their first three No. 1 records the same way. They were all up-tempo. Next I wanted a ballad.

The fourth consecutive No. 1 record, "I'll Be There," was done by Hal Davis, Willie Hutch, Bob West and me. We knew it was a hit when Michael's little sincere voice came out there singing to his girlfriend: [*singing*] "You and I must make a pact; we will bring Salvation back."

BB: *In the modern record business, the phrase "artist-development" is like a mantra. But back in the '60s, Motown was one of the first record companies to think like that. Whose idea was the artist development department, the "kick, turn and smile" school? And which artists fought the most against the idea of going through that process?*

BG: I never heard the term "kick, turn and smile" school, for one thing. My sisters Gwen and Anna had been pushing me to have a department to develop artists.

I don't know who fought the most. That was not one of the departments that I personally was involved in. In fact, I fought against it for a long time.

BB: *Did the artists understand what you were trying to achieve by having them play the Copa and Las Vegas? In his autobiography, Smokey says he was miserable playing places like that.*

BG: Vegas had a mesmerizing effect on us, this little company in Detroit. I always was kind of reaching out for Vegas, reaching out for Broadway, for the movies, while staying in my thing. I wanted more, I wanted a bigger picture. So Vegas was the way to get it—and the Supremes were the group to lead us that way, because they could do standards better than anybody and they had the image. So I was banking on them.

When the Supremes played the Copa—and everybody's dream was to play the Copa—we all got caught up in the thing that you had to be different, that our music wasn't good enough for places like that. We hadn't realized how important our music was; none of us had ever been to the Copa.

When the Supremes went in there, they did their hits, but then I added these great Broadway tunes that they did so well—and they were a smash.

All the artists who went in after that, they wanted to do what the Supremes had done. Marvin went into his "Me and My Shadow" stuff. It didn't work. Smokey [and the Miracles] went in, and they came on in these matador outfits singing "Poinciana." They weren't that great either.

I was trying to make the point that they should go in and do their stuff. Because by that time, I had finally come to my senses. After the Miracles, Tom Jones came in and played the Copa, doing Motown-type stuff—and he tore the place up!

After that, we realized Motown had become universal, that it had become something that [our artists] need never be ashamed of. I was never ashamed of it, but I realized I had fallen into the trap of thinking like that.

BB: *You also signed artists like Billy Eckstine. Why?*

BG: I was always trying to branch out into new kinds of music. That's why it was easy for Marvin to come out with his ballads. Even though I would want to push the Motown sound, I always liked Broadway, always liked movies, and I tried at different times to do different things. I brought in Sammy Davis at one time . . .

BB: *. . . and Tony Martin, Barbara McNair . . .*

BG: I was always trying to expand, but when I would expand and start losing my base, I'd have to get back. But Billy Eckstine was great, he had a couple of nice records [with Motown].

Ron Miller did a record with him called "Down to Earth." Ron and I had a problem with the lyrics, we were fighting, and he refused to change them. The phrase at the end of the song [should have been] "with me." He would not put it in. I said, "You can't write, 'Down to earth/ Down to earth/Down to earth.' You've got to say, 'Down to earth/Down to earth/Down to earth . . . with me.' You've got to lock it in, you've got to show why I want you down to earth with me."

Ron wouldn't do it. I said, "OK," although I thought that change would have made a big difference in the record.

BB: *Always the teacher.*

BG: I think the main thing in looking at my life is that I love bringing out potential in others. To do that, you've got to teach.

The whole thing was based on love. The people at Motown knew I loved them. They knew me very well; the outsiders didn't.

Even today, they love me. But they may be tempted to write bad things about me, because that's about me. Many artists have come to me and said, "Hey, I want to publish a book, but if I don't write something bad about you and the company, they'll never publish it."

It's a sad society where you cannot get published unless you say something negative, unless you lie. I can understand people wanting sensationalism, because I'm no different. But when it makes you do things that are abominable, when you can attack someone who's worked all his life to build something, when you would tear it down because someone says you'll make money if you do that . . . that's sad.

BB: *There always were some pretty weird rumors about Motown: that you were owned by the Mafia, for example. You have some fun in the book with that, and how [Motown sales chief] Barney Ales used to handle it.*

BG: Barney never really minded that too much, because, you know, we got our money a little quicker from distributors! I was screaming about [the rumors], yet there were people who said to me, "Boy, you're awful cool. Man, you get away with this stuff and other Mafia figures are getting caught."

Young black cats would come to me and say, "You're a bad dude, baby, you can get away with it." I'd say, "You don't understand, I'm not [in the Mafia]." Anyway, Barney was quite a character.

BB: *So much has been written about Motown over the years —a lot of it negative—but you've publicly said very little, until now. Why?*

BG: When I was building the company, I had a vision to move forward, and I was smart enough not to let those little obstacles stop me. When a football player's running down the field with the ball tucked under his arm and he stops to fight an obstacle, then someone else is going to get him. So he's got to outrun his obstacles. That's what I tried to do.

A lot of things hurt me. But I kept [the football image] in mind and let them go. When I sold the company, then I said to myself, "OK, now what's important to me in life?" It's a legacy and a body of work, and it's people who had confidence in us from the beginning, who want to know the real story. "Did I cheat the artists? Was I in the Mafia? Did I do this, did I do that?"

So here's the story, let me tell what it is, then I'm through with it. Then maybe I won't mind as much what people might say.

It's so ironic [*laughs*], because the reason I got into the business in the first place was because I couldn't get paid as a songwriter. When I couldn't get my money from the New York publishers, I thought, first of all, it's unfair, and not only that, it's bad business. If these people go out of business after two or three years because they don't pay people, they can never achieve longevity.

So I thought, if I pay all these people, they'll be stampeding through my door. And so Smokey got paid, and [other] people got paid—and they did stampede through my door. I had an instant publishing company, Jobete, which has lasted 30 years. Other companies have come and gone which you can't even remember. Why? Because I paid the artists.

Now, the book is finished, and I'm sitting up here, I pick up *Newsweek*, I read that Jackie Wilson and Mary Wells, two Motown artists, died broke. They talk about exploitation by white companies and they use me [as an example] that black companies do it, too. That was too much to bear. Jackie Wilson was never with Motown. Mary Wells left in 1964 with a No. 1 record, "My Guy," and went to five other record companies before she died in 1992.

Even if I were still pursuing a goal, I might have stopped for that one. So that's what the book is about, that's what the last five years of my life have been about.

BB: *You say you don't regret selling Motown?*

BG: No, not at all. I'm very happy with the way I did it, because I put it in the hands of people I respect. That was the key thing.

BB: *You don't miss the wars, the battleground of the modern record business?*

BG: Oh, sure, I miss the creative aspects of it. But I can fill that void with a lot of other creative things. I can still produce. I'm very interested in executive-producing an album with Smokey. That would be one of my great joys. It would bring back some real great [feelings], and I've told Smokey to wait until after I've finished promoting the book. He has written some incredible songs, and I'm really excited about working with him on them.

BB: *Do you listen to much current music? Rap, for example, or the new generation of vocal groups such as Boyz II Men, who are clearly based on the Temptations?*

BG: I listen to a lot: jazz, pop, blues, rap and whatever happens to be on the radio at the time I'm listening. As far as rap is concerned, some of it amazes me, it's so brilliant. Some I don't understand at all.

I think Boyz II Men relate to their peer group much the same way the Temps related to theirs when they started. They are expressing themselves in the same way that the youngsters today express themselves.

That's the affinity that allows them to be successful and so popular.

BB: *What about the women? There's a universe of difference between Queen Latifah or Mary J. Blige and, say, Mary Wells and Martha Reeves.*

BG: I'm not sure there is such a great difference. In many ways, Mary with her raspy voice, and Martha with her down-home, soulful stuff, are not unlike Queen Latifah. It's just that in this time and place, women are freer now and can be the protesters just like the men. In Mary's and Martha's time, it was neither fashionable, desirable nor interesting to have them do so, where now it is. But musically and vocally, hey, they're on top.

BB: *Is there a single record you'd want Motown to be remembered by, if it were a matter of putting just one in a time capsule for future historians?*

BG: No. Because it was a body of work. It was the legacy of what it meant in terms of what we did, how we did it and why we did. There's no one record that can capture the spirit and the meaning of what Motown was all about.

Just the Music: The Diana Ross Interview
David Nathan

BILLBOARD: *What were the earliest musical influences you recall?*

DIANA ROSS: First of all, I think the foundation has to do with spiritual music, church music, because that's wrapped around my family, my upbringing and early days. But it wasn't gospel performers. It wasn't professional people, it was just going to church. Then, during the late '50s, groups like the Chantels, the Shirelles, Frankie Lymon & The Teenagers . . . and Etta James with "Roll with Me Henry" . . . and there was one of her songs that was really emotional . . . "At Last" [No. 47 Pop, Billboard, 1961]. I used to go and see her at these little clubs in Detroit. I used to watch her, and I used to try and sing like her when I was little. I must have been 12 or 13 and I'd stand in front of the mirror singing "At Last."

BB: *When you and Mary Wilson and Florence Ballard began recording at Motown in 1960, what were those early sessions like?*

DR: Well, so much different than they are today. We had a two-track machine. Before we started singing ourselves, we were trying to do background work for other artists at

Originally published in *Billboard Magazine,* October 23, 1993.

the company, so those were exciting times, because it was just about really feeling the music and doing a lot of "oohs" and "aahs." I can remember where everything was set up in the room, "The Studio." It was just a very small room, and looking back, we didn't think it was so special then . . . we were just doing what we were doing. [When we began recording as the Supremes] it was about emoting out there, like you had to really get into it, behind the microphone, and of course there were no "punch-ins"! But it was really a new experience for us, because we'd never really sung a song and had it put on tape.

BB: *All of the early Supremes hits were written by Holland-Dozier-Holland . . .*

DR: Brian Holland seemed to be the musical part of the team. He played piano, and he played with a lot of feeling, a lot of soul . . . you know, he just had this special way with the piano, and he seemed to be the one who knew a lot about what was happening musically. He first came up with the song "I Hear a Symphony," and he listened to all types of music. Eddie Holland was the most organized of those two brothers, although I also knew that he was also very involved with the lyric writing. In fact, I think all three of them contributed to the lyrics. What Lamont seemed to be able to do was come up with those little licks, those hooks, the background parts. It was really a special unit. Eddie Holland was a good singer himself, so he would always show me how the songs would go, how to

do them. We didn't really have demos to work from then
. . . you'd just go in the studio with the piano and learn the
song, and sometimes the words were still being written
right there [in the studio].

BB: *It seems that Motown was one of the first companies—
and the Supremes one of the first pop groups—to do "concept" albums, like* We Remember Sam Cooke, A Little Bit
of Liverpool *and* Country & Western and Pop, *etc. . . .*

DR: Motown was an idea-oriented company. Berry
Gordy used to have these morning meetings, and they
were like brainstorming sessions. They just kept us all
ahead of what was going on. Someone was always aware
of what was going on in the charts, what records were selling, what the hits were. I give Berry a lot of the credit for
being able to be a visionary for the Supremes and his other
artists. He had an incredible sense, and he had such
a charisma about him, and he had the ability to hire
talented people—not just the creative people like the
performers and the songwriters and musicians—but he
also brought in incredible business people to be involved
with Motown in those early days.

BB: *How do you feel now about those early Supremes hits?*

DR: I realize how really good they were. In putting
together the four-CD set for my 30th anniversary, we
listened back to "Reflections," which is a very unusual

sound . . . then, looking back at "Love Child," "I'm Livin' in Shame" and the different style of things we did. I've always liked to sing songs that I really identify with and understand, and I started to really know that's what I really liked when we were doing "I'm Livin' in Shame." I said, "This is not about me," and they said, "Yeah, but every song you do doesn't have to be about you." But I said, "Yes, but you know, I want to feel like I can believe my songs . . . " So I basically had to kind of think in terms of acting when I was doing that . . .

BB: *Is there any particular song from the Supremes period that holds a special significance for you?*

DR: I'll tell you, almost every song. Through the short 10-year span that I spent with the Supremes—it was actually kind of a short span, you know—we did a tremendous amount of work in 10 years, and there was always something going on about each song, whether it was doing it on an Ed Sullivan Show or being in Las Vegas or doing it in the studio. For me, "Someday We'll Be Together" was an amazing song to find right at that moment when the Supremes were breaking up. It was a very, very emotional time, and it was a wonderful song, written by Johnny Bristol. I actually recorded the song really with some other girls. It was not the Supremes in the background . . .

BB: *How did you feel about leaving the Supremes and launching your solo career?*

DR: I had spent 10 years building up a name, an image and a relationship, and we had become successful. It's just like walking away from a successful business: you wonder if you can have the same success, but it was a change that just had to happen. I couldn't have stayed where I was. So the fear was, will I be OK? Will my records be hits? People had done some of the same things and weren't successful. Mary Wells left Motown and went to other record companies and tried and nothing had materialized. The first year maybe it turns out all right, then after that you wonder if it's going to keep going. When you make a decision to make a split, you need to take responsibility that what happens you've caused and you've created. I think at that time, I was mature enough to know that this might not work. It's like leaving, going through a doorway into the darkness . . . and you don't really know what's out there. Who knows, the Supremes could have gone on to be a success and I could have maybe had a couple of records out, and then if it didn't work, how long will record companies stick with you? They don't always, and it's really about the artists who make the money for the company.

BB: *Nick Ashford and Valerie Simpson worked on your [1970] debut album. What memories do you have about that project?*

DR: Berry Gordy called Nick and Val in and wanted them to write for me, so they in turn started planning the album. I wasn't checked in with, like, "Which songs do you want to have?" and that kind of thing. They just put together the songs, and we went in and did the album. I just loved working with the two of them because they're so talented. "Ain't No Mountain High Enough" was just so inspirational, and we recorded that in L.A., not in Detroit at the normal Motown studios. I also did "Reach Out and Touch" in L.A., and I remember what was going on at the time I recorded the song. My brother was going through a real difficult time, so it was a very emotional and personal song for me. I was thinking a lot about my brother in the session. You know, some songs you take very, very personally, and some are taken personally in a more exterior, rather than interior, kind of way.

BB: *How would you characterize those early years in your solo career?*

DR: I was really going through major changes in my life. You know, there are peak points where you're having a real learning experience and a real change, real trusting of yourself. A lot of things were happening in the '70s, and I think in a sense it was frightening, leaving the girls, but there was a freedom, a freeing of myself. I was beginning to trust myself more as a singer and getting much more confidence and that may have shown through too. That whole time was just really fast . . . I would be out on tour and we started finding record studios in different places. One of the most exciting parts of that was watching how Berry stayed on top of the producers, stayed on top of

pulling all these pieces together . . . because we were doing the doing and they were doing the thinking.

BB: *When you first started recording as a solo artist, Mar-*
vin Gaye was coming out with What's Going On. *Stevie*
Wonder was starting to produce himself. Did any of what
was going on with either of them musically in any way affect
you as a recording artist?

DR: I'm sure that somewhere deep inside I was wanting to
express myself musically as well, but I'm not a musician. I
always had to rely on someone else finding a song. I could
help with lyrics and words and the feel, but I wasn't a songwriter, where I could go to a piano. And what I was doing
was working for me. I wanted to express my feelings about
what was going on in the world in my music . . . but we were
kind of kept in this "nice" bag . . . But there was a lot going
on at the time, big, incredible changes . . . and everybody
was full and wanted to express that. I was sort of in a box
during that time, not able to put that kind of music on tape
because that's not what was expected of me, it was not my
image and all that . . . so I was kinda torn.

BB: *You did produce "Imagine" and "Save the Children/*
Brown Baby" on your Touch Me in the Morning *album* . . .

DR: That was my way of talking about my feelings, the
things I was thinking about. I was having babies and I
wanted to do some songs for my children.

BB: *Speaking of Marvin Gaye, you also recorded an album with him. What was that experience like for you?*

DR: At first, it was wonderful working with Marvin. He was such a mysterious person—loving, very sensitive for a man. But I found it hard to work with him in the studio, so we started singing separately. We did the first couple of things together and then . . . I'll tell you . . . because he used to smoke grass in the studio, and I didn't want to be in there. At one time, I was pregnant, I remember saying distinctly, "If you want to do this, do it outside."

BB: *At what point did you start to have some influence over what you recorded as a solo artist?*

DR: Probably not until I left Motown! Not until I went to RCA. I was a pretty well-directed artist, so they didn't bring anything to me that was so awful. I remember Suzanne de Passe bringing me "Love Hangover," and she had to make me believe in the song because it wasn't ex-actly a song . . . I mean, it was a lot of improvising, it was all "feel," it was all "feeling." It was like the beginning of the disco, kinda dance things . . . she played it to me in my kitchen, and I kept saying, "yeah, but . . . " Then I went in the studio and did it in one take . . . it was all ad-lib, every little thing . . . When I do "If there's a cure for this," it's like Billie Holiday, I put everything that I was feeling at the time into it . . . and I was thinking about Billie Hol-iday and *Lady Sings the Blues,* which we had just done . . .

BB: *How did* Lady *and* Mahogany *affect your musical career?*

DR: Music has always been there throughout my whole career, especially with *Lady Sings the Blues.* It was a very important musical piece. What that did was to have a different kind of influence on my voice and who I was. Because then I started realizing that there was another way of giving my feelings out, you know, through jazz. I started doing research into jazz a little bit more. I wanted to know, "What is jazz?" "What is improvising?" I would go and listen to a lot of early time jazz artists. Berry Gordy was into jazz, and he would sit down and show me what jazz was about and count out the bars . . . I wanted to understand the difference between jazz and blues and how they merged and all of that. "Do You Know Where You're Going To," that came from *Mahogany.* I was doing the film and, you know, you're just wondering, is your life working? It's six years later after the Supremes and I'm still trying to find out where I'm going to be . . .

BB: *And then* The Wiz, *working with Quincy Jones* . . .

DR: Well, he's an extreme professional, and most of the time I was in the studio with Quincy, Michael Jackson was there, and we enjoyed the work and had a lot of fun. It was a great experience because Quincy knows exactly what he wants.

BB: *You had two very successful albums at the end of your first 10 years as a solo artist at Motown:* The Boss *and* diana. *What are your thoughts about those records?*

DR: *The Boss* was done (with Nick Ashford and Valerie Simpson) as a complete album. It wasn't like a concept record, but I selected the songs and I was taking a little more responsibility . . . I was fighting a lot to have a voice in choosing the material. I think *The Boss* still sounds really good . . . and I remember when I did the high part at the end of the song, everybody thought that wasn't me, that it was somebody else!

Working with Nile Rodgers and Bernard Edwards [producers of *diana*] was really a good experience because by that time I had moved to New York and I'd put my kids in school there. I had also gone through the things you go through in your life . . . I think people start making changes in their lives when they feel dissatisfied. I was really making changes in my life right at that time. That's when I met Nile and Bernard: we were talking about all of this . . . then they went away and wrote about all the things I was saying. I felt like I was "coming out" and my life was "upside down." I think about the only song on there that probably did not have an identification with me was "My Old Piano."

BB: *You also worked with Lionel Richie on the duet "Endless Love" just before he left the Commodores and launched his solo career . . .*

DR: Lionel wasn't there much during the recording process. [Producer] James Carmichael was there most of the time, and James really has this incredible ear . . . and it was hard work, everything had to be just right for him, but I liked that. I felt like I was really learning something from him. Lionel was launching his solo career around that time, and I think the company wanted me to do the duet with him because in a sense, it was like a launching pad for him . . .

BB: *You left Motown in 1980 and signed with RCA. How was that for you?*

DR: It was really tremendously hard . . . I was in New York and had three little babies to be responsible for. There was a lot going on, a lot of things, some of which I can't really talk about at this time . . . It was important for me to stand on my own two feet and . . . people started to change. Things were different, the business was different. Motown was no longer in Detroit . . . the people trying to give directions were not the people from the beginning. People were telling me what to do, and I didn't know who they were. Berry was always very busy, setting up his company out in California. The [Motown] family relationship was really gone . . .

BB: *You chose RCA . . .*

DR: We didn't check at many different companies . . . just a few of the top companies. I met [then-president] Bob

Summer, who I liked very much, and I got a brand new deal with RCA. It wasn't just the financial part of the deal: I was able to also produce my own things and be involved in every aspect of recording, the artwork, the selection of people I worked with. Some of those things weren't easy for me to do at Motown. Everything was already set up and planned before, and they had been doing this so much that they didn't want to relinquish those controls . . .

BB: *The early years at RCA . . .*

DR: Fantastic . . . I was writing my own songs . . . When I signed with RCA, when I started on my own, I got to know every musician. It was like there was a relationship there. I got to know the people who did the arrangements and worked with them, learned to mix, and I was at the mastering session, I went over to Sterling Sound and built a relationship with people there. I think people think you go in and you sing and then you're done. Well, maybe in the early days it was that way, but to be involved in the material all the way was just wonderful.

BB: *When did you first start writing songs?*

DR: Well, I've always written things, but no one ever took my writing seriously. In the '60s and early '70s, nobody looked at my songs; they weren't really songs so much as ideas and sort of poetry, my thoughts. So there were things that I had written way back in the early days . . . but I said, "OK, I'm not even going to try and be a songwriter, it's silly for me to try and do everything, I'll just do what I do and interpret some of these great songwriters" . . .

I just started to want to put my feelings on paper more, whether it was a love song or just a little ditty or something. The first thing I did was "Work That Body." I always worked with other writers who played the piano, and many times I worked with writers and didn't put my name to any songs because it wasn't necessary . . .

BB: *Your first RCA hit was the Frankie Lymon classic, "Why Do Fools Fall in Love" . . .*

DR: That was the first song I used to sing with the Supremes. It was the song I auditioned for Motown with—that and the Drifters' "There Goes My Baby."

BB: *Michael Jackson wrote "Muscles" for you, right?*

DR: I just called and asked him would he write me a song, and he wrote "Muscles," and I didn't know it was about a snake. I thought it was about muscles!

BB: *What are your thoughts about the RCA years?*

DR: That I was really trusted by the company. I delivered my albums to them completed. I did the artwork, everything. It began to be a much more personalized experience. I selected the music, the songs that were written for me . . . I would call publishers direct to find material. Also, I had created my management company at that time [1981], I had my own offices, secretaries, the whole setup. We had our own tiny little Motown, with publishing companies [Rossville and Rosstown]. When you start setting up your own company, having a logo and stationery designed, then you know you're grown-up . . .

BB: *You left RCA in 1987 . . .*

DR: My contract was up, but they had changed manpower there. Bob Summer was no longer there, new people had come in, and the truth is, they didn't value me. It really felt like they were into this new, young crop, whoever was coming up at the time. I remember thinking I need to be somewhere where people would be happy to have me. And the records hadn't been hits at the end of those years and again, it's about making money. If you're not making money for a record company . . .

BB: *So you returned to Motown . . .*

DR: MCA was interested in me, and I never thought I was going to go back to Motown. Somewhere, in the meantime, Berry sold the company to MCA, and they were buying it with the thought that some of the artists on MCA would move to Motown. I'd already made the deal with MCA when they approached me. They said, "We'd like you to be on Motown," but I didn't know.

I had a lot of thoughts about it, so I said, "If I come back to the company, I would like to come back in the capacity of being more than just the artist. I would like to try to be the keeper of the flame to keep Motown the way it was in the early days, to be nurturing to the artists, to try to give them the wisdom that I had learned over these years." And that really is what [Motown president] Jheryl Busby wanted . . . to make Motown like it was, with new, young artists. I just wanted to be there to nurture it and be involved in that and try to make it the way it once was without it becoming the big kind of factory-like situation. That's what's missing in a lot of the big record companies . . .

BB: *How would you characterize the last few years at Motown?*

DR: It's been very much a grind. I stayed off work for about a year . . . I was having my babies, and I decided to do the album *Working Overtime* because I liked to watch BET on television, the dancers, the kids doing the hip-hop and so on . . . You know, I'm a risk-taker, and I don't want to just do what's expected . . . I just keep jumping out there, figuring out how to begin again and stay vital and alive and take chances. So I did that album and liked it very much. It did not do that well and probably could have done well if it had been promoted better. Even with Motown's name, it was still like a brand new company, a baby company, and a lot of things had to be worked out. Some business things seemed to interfere with marketing and promotion and getting the material out there and distributing it. I was caught in a little bit of that, but I think everyone's trying to pull together now. But when you start a business, I think it takes the first, almost seven years to get going . . .

BB: *And then you did a second album,* The Force behind the Power . . .

DR: I finally got my Stevie Wonder song, and that was the last song we got on the album. I went about my musical search, trying to get songs specifically written for me and just keep trying to find the good material, looking for the hit. You know, I listen to everything. People give me a tape in the market, and I'll listen to it because you don't know where the hit's coming from, you don't know where the good idea's gonna come from . . .

BB: *After* The Force behind the Power, *you did the* Stolen Moments *album, and now there's the 30th-anniversary boxed set,* Forever, Diana. *In closing, can you say a few words about putting that project together?*

DR: The idea for doing the boxed set came between my 25th and 30th anniversary, although it's probably more like 31 or 32 years since I first started. We based it on the release date of the Supremes' "When the Lovelight Starts Shining through His Eyes" in 1963. My approach, ever since I started working on this compilation, has been to try and make it really personal. That's why I was involved in every aspect of it, from selecting the songs to picking the photographs, writing the captions for the photos to doing the liner notes. I think personalizing it is so much nicer, and the boxed set is something directly from me to my fans.

Interview with Stevie Wonder

David Nathan

BILLBOARD: *I was going to start in a logical place, which was to talk about your new album—and we will talk about your new album, but I'm going to start in another place. There was a point in your career, probably around 1969 or 1970, where you seem to have made a conscious decision to address social issues. Can you say who or what inspired you at that time?*

STEVIE WONDER: I think that probably God has always used me as a vehicle, and that's the way I've seen it. At some point in time, it just came as a feeling to me that that was right to do. It wasn't like I said, "OK, I'm going to do this now." It just happened, and probably the public's first introduction to me doing it is in the song "Blowin' in the Wind" that I did with Clarence Paul as a duet. But obviously, things that were going on caused me to think and emote and ultimately write and express my feelings and point of view on the different issues that confront us in this society.

BB: *It seems as if it was more like an evolution in your thinking. Do you feel the first album to really express that was [1971's] Where I'm Coming From?*

Originally published in *Billboard Magazine*, May 13, 1995.

SW: Yeah, that definitely was the first album where it was me working with Syreeta [Wright] on different topics. That is the first album where you can see all that happening.

BB: *Can you recall if there were any particular conversations with people that led you toward developing that sort of social enlightenment?*

SW: I have to say that Vietnam was something that I was interested in, the racial situation that still existed, the violence that happened within the inner cities, the fact of the psychological and emotional state of the people. I think even with a song like "Take up a Course in Happiness" [from *Where I'm Coming From*], I was saying that there are going to be problems in life. There are going to be highs and lows, and you have to work with dealing with them and not giving up. Obviously, that song—and there were other songs too—dealt with that kind of topic. "Look Around" was kind of dealing with the space situation. "Think of Me as Your Soldier" is dealing with someone who has an endless love for someone.

But if you look at, say, [the 1972 album] *Music of My Mind,* you don't really see that many of those kinds of songs on there. You have "Girl Blue," which is a song about someone abusing themselves or allowing themselves to be abused . . . "Evil," which is kind of a song that deals with asking the questions, "Why do you break so many hearts? Why have you caused such havoc and destruction in this world of ours?" There have been so many different inspirations for so many songs.

Based on situations that we have all seen, or that I've seen, those kinds of things are inspired by experiencing life, experiencing people in life and different circumstances that people either put themselves in or put other people through.

BB: *So I assume a lot of inspiration then came from discussing things with people, as well as from your own experiences.*

SW: Definitely. Exactly. And from listening to the radio, television, the news, books and all the different things that evoke or cause thoughts and feelings about situations or conditions.

BB: *Did you consider at that juncture that what you were doing musically was risky [at the time]? Were you aware of being rather cutting edge, or were you simply expressing yourself?*

SW: I knew that maybe it was risky, but I didn't really think of that as being a reason I should stop. I thought it was more important for me to express those things, to deal with those topics that were not only on my mind but heavy on my heart. I basically believe that these were and are issues we need to deal with, that need to be confronted. That, if in fact through people hearing about these things, it may bring a thought to their mind. With the song "Front Line" [from the 1982 album *Original Musiquarium I*], about "Agent Orange," for those people to not have gotten the medical attention is a travesty to what we say we are all about. So I was very disappointed, and the way you express disappointment or concern is you talk about it. I didn't feel you were supposed to keep it quiet—"Don't say anything and let it go on"—like let people go through their pains and you make your money, and forget about it.

BB: *The other artists I'm thinking about from around that time who took on similar themes are Marvin Gaye with* What's Going On? *and Curtis Mayfield, Nina Simone and James Brown. Did they influence you in terms of your thinking?*

SW: Definitely. Their music inspired me, and they wrote some great stuff. Marvin Gaye's *What's Going On?* is still one of the most incredible albums in the history of music. It was a record I loved, and it encouraged me. It encouraged me more than it influenced me, because it said there was another person not willing to sacrifice his art because it may not be a popular topic of the day. Like "[Inner City Blues] Makes Me Wanna Holler" . . . "natural fact is, I can't pay my taxes . . ." And we are all confronted with it throughout the world.

Taxes are high in the United States, and they are high in Great Britain. The bad thing about it is that taxes are getting high and the conditions need to be changed, and the things we should be spending our money on, to make a change for the better, [the politicians] are saying, "It's too much money, we need to cut money from the budget in education." You get someone like Gingrich . . . I made an analogy last night: I said, "Some politicians are like record execs, because what happens is you have some record execs who have positions and they say, 'Hey, you should do this, this is the thing that is happening,' and it's only because they may have heard of it, but they wouldn't know hip-hop from be-bop. You may do it, and they then say, 'This is not happening.' It's the same with politicians: they say, 'Look, this is what we need to do, we need to cut here.' Yet the position they take will ultimately do nothing for the well-being of society." That's the analogy that I made. . . .

BB: *A lot of people consider you one of the pioneers on the synthesizer, since you were so instrumental in making that instrument popular. How do you feel about your reputation in that regard?*

SW: I feel good, in the sense that maybe through the way that I used it—as a tool to work with sounds I had in my mind (since I couldn't do notation and give a musician the part to do)—I could play keyboards enough to play that part and thus give the musicians a sense of the things I wanted from them. From the very beginning, synthesizers were used—on a lot of the scary movies and then obviously on the Beach Boys' "Good Vibrations." I felt good that I was able to take [inspiration] from a place where great work was done—by Wendy Carlos, who did *Switched on Bach* and *Clockwork Orange*.

There were those musicians who were just into it. Marvin Gaye, for instance, on "Mercy Mercy Me," and I think some of the other stuff on that album. Motown had a Moog synthesizer, probably the same one he used, but no one really worked with it. Then more and more people began to use it. Emerson, Lake, and Palmer did some great stuff that kind of moved the synthesizer to another place. Malcolm [Cecil] and Bob [Margouleff] were there and they did some great stuff. Various synthesists have brought it a long way, and I feel very happy that I was able to take it to another place and get it from just being some fun little gadget that people could mess with and find that there is something to actually come out of it that gives a writer a whole other spectrum to use when arranging. Nowadays, I feel the same way about the computer.

BB: *As a songwriter, with your body of work, there is an enormous amount of music there, there are great songs. What is your basic way of writing or approaching a song? Do you get an idea and put it down to develop later, or how do you typically work?*

SW: The basic idea and the melody usually come to me first. Then the music for the verses. . . .

BB: *There have always been rumors that you have thousands of songs that you haven't completed. Is that true?*

SW: I have a lot of songs in different stages. I kept it like that. I probably, probably, probably will finish more of them and still put them aside, so that whenever I leave this planet, my children will still be here. And my wife.

BB: *So you'd be leaving a legacy?*

SW: Yeah, leaving it for them.

BB: *Do you go back and work on songs?*

SW: Of course. If I write a song and I don't immediately put it down on tape, I might forget it for a day, but it will fortunately come back to me. That happens from time to time. It's a trip, because if you don't put it down, you might lose it . . . I do have a lot of songs and I hope that I don't finish all the songs that I write in my lifetime. I have a couple of thousand, maybe more.

BB: *Do you revisit them very often?*

SW: Yes, like with "My Love Is with You," that's an older song, I had the basic idea and melody [for some time]. The idea originally was dealing with a love thing, you know, like "My love is with you wherever you are." It was so long, and I wasn't doing anything with it, and then I thought of it in a whole other way. I always feel that when that happens it's like a blessing from God.

BB: *On a practical basis, do you have all the songs you've ever begun, in different stages, catalogued in some way? If you need to go find a tape of something that you started writing 19 years ago . . .*

SW: Catalogued enough for me. . . .

BB: *Do you go back and listen to your older music?*

SW: Yes.

BB: *And when you listen, what inspires you? What gets you excited again?*

SW: I'm inspired if I can still listen and feel the same emotions. It lets me know that I'm still in the same place about how I feel about those different things. Like "Visions" [from 1973's *Innervisions*] for instance. Or *Songs in the Key of Life*, songs from that [1976].

BB: *Is there a particular album for you that you would consider to be a milestone?*

SW: *Songs in the Key of Life*. It was also a kind of pivotal point of those kinds of albums. I had done *Music of My Mind* [1972], *Talking Book* [1972], *Innervisions, Fulfill-*

ingness' First Finale [1974] and then *Songs in the Key of Life.* . . .

BB: *Do you ever get tired of touring?*

SW: I like traveling. It's been no problem for me.

BB: *Do you still enjoy performing?*

SW: Yes, I do, very much so. I love performing.

BB: *What do you think of the current music scene? What are your thoughts about the music you're hearing on the radio?*

SW: I like a lot of the music that's out. I like a lot of the rap groups. I like some of the hip-hop stuff, the R&B stuff. I don't have any problem with any of that. What I don't like is probably the fact that programming for these stations is limiting the spectrum of the public's appreciation for music. It's not broad enough. You've got stations that have bought other stations and there's two different formats happening. It's a funny thing. In one sense. I miss the "variety shows" because with the shows like *Ed Sullivan,* you might see someone like Jackie Wilson or The Jackson Five, and then along with that you might see a trampoline act or a violinist of 16 or 15 or 12 years of age. You might see a dancer who does some incredible stuff, or an opera singer. It gave kids more of an appreciation for music and for art. . . .

What's Really Going On with Marvin Gaye?

SEPIA: *What is your new music all about?*

MARVIN GAYE: There is a theme to it and the theme is the war between the sexes.

SP: *Where do you see this war coming from?*

MG: I see it coming from the nature of woman from the very beginning. And I see it all coming back. Her nature is rising, her colors are beginning to show again, just as they always have throughout history. But ultimately she will always come back to the realization that man is superior to her, and chosen first, and he will always have that status no matter what she thinks.

SP: *How do you figure that?*

MG: Mother Nature has ways of dealing with over-population. The trouble with man is that he is always attempting to control things. This isn't his thing, this is God's thing and all he has to do is be cool and it'll work out. To give you an example, Mother Nature will come up with plagues, heaven forbid, and the weak will have to go. She'll straighten out her population problems; she knows

Originally published in *Sepia* 27, no. 4 (April 1978): 14–22.

how. She keeps things under control, and all we do is mess with it, and do ridiculous things. Natural law and natural order should be adhered to and respected. Woman has to respect her position and come to know what God really requires of her, what her job and what her purpose is. Once she understands that, she'll not be happy with it because she'll feel that ours is easier, and ours is more aggressive, and she'll become jealous of that. It's not my fault that she took the apple off the tree. Don't get mad at me. I didn't pick the apple; ya know what I mean. You did it; I'm sorry, but God isn't as happy with you as He is with me. So He said that you will bear the pain of childbirth. You shouldn't have got the apple. So you're upset 'cause you've got to be careful and you've got to watch what you're doin'. Well, listen, you've got to do right, and if you don't do right you're gonna run into trouble because He knows the nature of you. Put this on yourself or be cool. So, now you're going to invent a pill where you can do it anyway as much as you want to and a man doesn't have to worry. When you go back and look at everything, and read the Bible 'cause it seems that that's the way it went down pretty much, there are a few things you might want to question. But, for the most part, it's pretty much there. And, for the most part, women are pretty much the way they've always been.

SP: *What do you feel about women's demands, women's liberation, and the so-called independent woman?*

MG: Man is pretty weak, I think, in these terms, to allow himself to bow to some of the demands of the more radical women of today. Not even are they afraid to bend, but they're even afraid to talk about it and express their views. It's not chauvinistic to tell the truth. It may hurt to recognize it, but I'm the King. And I love you and you're the Queen, and God said that, and the Queen cannot be the King, the Queen must be the Queen and the King must be the King. Though I just probably lost a couple of million sales.

SP: *Who is to blame?*

MG: Men have overdone their roles and have not lived up to their expectations as men. It's our fault, basically. I would say that women are stronger than men today, especially mentally. Physically they are really asserting themselves, and I'm being shocked every day by the physical prowess of women. Men should really get themselves together, and become real men again or we will be in trouble. I know that if we're on our jobs, a woman can respect that and take her rightful place as a woman, if a man is really a man. When a man is really a man, he knows what it is to be a man and the responsibility of being a real man, he assumes that responsibility, and the woman can only respect it.

SP: *Is that how things are working in your new relationship?*

MG: No, it isn't. My young lady's caught up in the Movement, with the philosophy of it, and I'm rather old-fashioned in thinking. And we have some problems in that area, but I am the ram and I shall survey at all costs. I'm 17 years older than she is. I'm 38.

SP: *What has brought Marvin Gaye back out in terms of both performing and recording live albums?*

MG: That young woman . . . a young lady. Her name is Janis Hunter. She's helped to help me regain my sense of youth, and my spirit and my love for my music.

SP: *If you weren't a musician, what would Marvin Gaye be?*

MG: After football, my third choice in life would have probably been to be an attorney, a good one, a noble one, a rarity.

SP: *Do you think this new romantic affair has brought out parts of you that you kept hidden?*

MG: I'm very much in love with her, and being very much in love with someone will bring out a lot of things. She inspires me in a lot of areas that I might not have been inspired. I know about trying to accomplish something in life and not knowing really what it is you're trying to accomplish; but, I do know that I am going to accomplish something phenomenal. I know that. It is my belief that if you can find someone that you can live with and who inspires you, it's all for the better, and she adds a lot of inspiration to me.

SP: *Would you say your previous marriage put a cynical vibe on you?*

MG: I'm really having the same battle with her that my ex-wife had with me, and that is a struggle for identity and power that is recognizable and one that is adhered to. I refuse to be what I felt in my heart, less than a man. Control and power and that sort of thing, and being a very strong woman, she probably needed a man who is not a ram, some headstrong person, 'cause I'm very heady.

SP: *Do you choose all your directions?*

MG: I choose my directions and take my battles as they come. I feel I'm a greater warrior for them if I win, and I feel I've won most of my battles. I've had my heart ache many times, but it only makes you stronger if you are of a strong body and mind. It can only temper you for the big battles you have later in life. Everybody must go through them. So although I would have preferred that we could have seen things differently as it is in most affairs of the heart, unless two people have tremendous understanding and tremendous foundation. Generally, you'll find that there are a lot of problems.

SP: *Do you feel you're now more in control of the direction you want to be moving in?*

MG: Well, this business of control and ego and power and having what you want and doing what you want with it, is all very well and good, but I've found that once you acquire it, there isn't a great deal of satisfaction in it, and you'll find that being on your own and having the control in your hands is a great responsibility and if you're not ready to handle it you're better off leaving things in the hands of those who are able to control it, and handle the power of a situation.

SP: *Is Marvin Gaye ready?*

MG: Personally, I feel I'm ready, I feel I've been ready for many years. I am happy now with my working conditions at Motown Records. I am not happy with the business.

SP: *How so?*

MG: I feel like . . . this business is strange because if you are an artist and you adhere strictly to the guidelines of what it's supposed to be to be an artist, then you don't cross out of this mold if you are truly an artist.

SP: *What is a true artist?*

MG: The fact you can even die from it or starve to death. I am true to my art, I am true to my music, I am true to the guardian angel of artists and I pay my homage to Her or Him whatever kind of sex it is. I try and respect It; I know It's good to me, so I have to be true. The thing is then if your have all this power placed in your hands, it's rather impossible in the way the world is geared economically. Today in our system of government, you would be a complete idiot if you got all involved in the politics of running a big corporate operation when you need to be relaxed and not worry about anything else. You just have to believe that the Guardian Angel will protect you, and if you've been wronged, She will avenge or She'll take the message on to God's avenger and He'll take care of it.

SP: *What about business vs. art?*

MG: Be an artist, strictly an artist, and whatever wealth and fame you receive is earned and is blessed and is yours. I don't like to put out a lot of records and albums just because record companies want a lot of material in bulk. I mean that, to me, that is too commercial. I want to put out something that says something, something that you can feel. Well, I would become unfeeling after a while if I just had to use me up time and again. I couldn't put any energy in, any heart, any tears, any love, any whatever emotion I want to put in, because I wouldn't have time to re-energize. I mean you soon run out. There's only so much in this world that you can write and sing about. It's the same thing over and over again, anyway; and, to me, it gets a little boring sometimes.

SP: *What is Marvin Gaye truly concerned with?*

MG: I think that what I am basically concerned with is being a true artist, and it's difficult. You have to be intelligent to be a true artist, 'cause you will definitely be exploited beyond any reasonable expectations. But still you have to remain an artist and the fight and struggle is a very difficult one that you really have to have grips on yourself, what you believe in, how far you will bend, and you have to stick to that and trust that the Guardian Angels will bring you through as they have always with me. To me, the hardest thing about being an artist is having the control to put out your art.

SP: *Again—so many true artists never get their just financial rewards.*

MG: Yes, this is 'cause there are many deals made with your product, and nobody thinks that an artist . . . I mean when I put out a record, that to me is my painting, and it saddens me to see it merchandised and handled and deals made. It really saddens me. Of course I make a lot of money and everything on it. That isn't the first priority, though; that's not number one. Like I say, if it's good and you're a good artist and you're true to your work the money will come, the fame will come, all that will come, just hang in there strong and these forces will bless you. It's got to happen, it's law, and it always works. Especially if you're talented and blessed with it.

SP: *Was Marvin Gaye put out here for a supreme reason?*

MG: In the first place, there are those of us here who were put here with certain talents and we were put here so we could keep the people happy, keep their heads and hearts strong, give them a release, a way to release the evil one. Music to play, to reminisce by, whatever the mood . . . music for love, music for work. We are very important people to people. I don't think we're really thought of in the right light because there are other people in the industry who are so commercial, and so commercially-minded that the artists are closed out; you can't even see a real artist anymore 'cause all record companies work the same way.

SP: *What kind of blatant commercialism exists?*

MG: Bulk exploitation, bulk commercialism, and get it out there, who can sell the most records and, you know, they're not coming from a place where there's a respect for the artists because there are other people who sing as well as an artist might, or produce as well as an artist might. He may be a man possessed with greed; the law still works for him, also. It might work in reverse, but there is nothing that says a man who works for greed can't be successful because he has talent, also. And especially if there's a machine set up there just going to push his record. So it's hard to say if the artist is the better of the two because he's more easily exploited because he's more apt to take concessions or make concessions, where the man of greed wouldn't.

SP: *Have you ever been exploited in your art?*

MG: I am very easily exploited because, when I'm giving up material, I'm giving up honesty, heart and soul and pure love. Pure love of my music and my respect, and I'm pouring it out when I'm doing something, or I won't do it. And when they get something from an artist, myself or any other artist in the business, then it is something special. I think it's something special, and I think there's a difference between stock stuff and stuff from people in this industry who have special talents and special gifts. They are special people.

SP: *Is it worth it?*

MG: Well, I don't think we're respected enough. Honor . . . I can't understand why an artist should be honored so much, but I certainly think that if people want to, it's beautiful, but I don't think that it's a prerequisite. But I do think that being very respectful and understanding that you are getting from this person and keeping this person happy and as healthy as possible and as protected as possible. I feel that artists are as important as, say, a President. Without them this would be an awful world.

SP: *How do you feel about a lot of acts catering to the craziness in society just to get over?*

MG: The artist has to make a living like anybody else. It's very simple; the record companies have decided that this is the vehicle by which the music shall reach the people. I have no control over that; that's a biggie. I mean, if this is the only vehicle, I have one choice. I can either be an artist and accept the fact that this is the only vehicle from which my music can reach the people, or I can say I don't like this vehicle and I don't like this business, and I don't like the way things are done to artists, and people, and the insides of it, and I just won't do anything. But, then, if I don't do anything, I also know that, on the other hand, if I'm thinking on a noble scale, that to use this vehicle, to really get a message out and across to people is also a great thing. Even though they're making a lot of money doing it, and heaven knows what they're doing with it. I mean I don't get a lot of it [*laughs*]. They do have an awful lot of overhead and stuff like that, and record companies probably don't make as much money as people think. They make a lot of money, but they probably don't make as much money as people feel they do. I still don't think that, in proportion to what the artist is giving, he makes nearly enough money from the total sales; after all, if you don't have anyplace to get it, and this is the source [*points at his chest*], then you're tapping the mine, and when the mine runs out, you simply go and get yourself another mine. What happens is you're a terrific mine, then they can tap you for years, and for that you deserve fantastic rewards, because you're a terrific mine and they may make money off this mine for many, many years. But on the other hand, if the mine is an artist, he doesn't want to be exploited, commercialized, merchandised, but this is their only way to make money because there are other record companies who are in competition with them and who are doing all these things. It's like you either play the game or you get eaten up. It's a vicious, vicious cycle.

SP: *Do you feel now that you and Motown Records have straightened out your differences?*

MG: Motown is probably a better record company, maybe not for some artists, but for me. If it wasn't for the total lunacy of the people in control, I would never leave this company because, at least, they understand me and I understand them. Over this period of years, we've worked out a pretty good relationship. I go nuts one time, and they go nuts the next, and we just all still go nuts together. Meanwhile the years keep passing and I hope that my career keeps going the way it's going. I'm a very patient man. I know that whatever is supposed to happen in life, I'll have it, as long as I keep my attitudes proper.

SP: *There was talk at one time that you and Stevie Wonder were going to have a record company together. It this true?*

MG: There again you're caught in the same old trap because we'll get eaten up too if we don't play the game the way the rest of the biggies are playing it. We couldn't possibly survive. So, for me, I realized after giving it a little thought, it would be a pretty hypocritical thing to do because I can't have my views on record companies and think that I'm going to have a record company that's going to be successful where I can do something other than what these big fellas are doing. So, I would rather never have a record company. I don't want to deal with it. I may have a label, a record label that Motown would distribute for me. But I could never be into the record manufacturing business. Never in my life. That would be like asking Michelangelo to sell everybody else's paintings. I can't do that; I can't sell records. How much would I charge? I mean, at least I feel a little better 'cause I don't put the price of $10 or $7 on it. I might sell it a bit cheaper myself; in fact, I'm sure I would.

SP: *That happened with a lot of white rock groups, like the Jefferson Airplane or the Grateful Dead. They'd get total control of their product, with their own labels.*

MG: It's very difficult to be show and business. It takes a hell of an artist to be the show and the business. You've really got to be intelligent, man. You've got be so smart and put a lot of time, energy, and guts into it. You really have to have it on the ball 'cause it's a lot easier to be the show and let someone else be the business. Or let somebody be the show while you do the business, I don't think I could ever handle the business, anyway. So, yes, my product would immediately show the result of my handling the business, because I would immediately start having fights with my inner self as an artist. And I certainly wouldn't be pure enough to produce anything that would be of fine quality.

I'd be having a war with myself and simply be telling a lie on wax. On the other hand, I would find that running the business side of things would keep me so preoccupied that I really wouldn't have time to give to put myself in the state to produce something really good. When you're hungry and you're noble and you go off into this business saying I want it, I want success, I want a hit . . . Then this thing says, OK you really want it, you're really gonna do it, right? And you say, 'Yeah, yeah, I'll do it.' And it lets you get a hit. Then, it watches you a little bit, watches you go down the road a bit and see what you get off into. People think that they are all everything, nobody's nothing.

SP: *How much is Marvin Gaye controlled?*

MG: Everything is controlled and so is everybody, and as soon as people start setting into the fact that what they cannot see, but what most of us can sense, is very real, and that is what we should play ball with: going on your feelings and intuitions rather than what someone tells you. I have this studio and it's good for me 'cause I can create and sit in it and the vibes are in the walls and in the music. I feel very good here in this; it's of music, it's about music. And, I imagine commercially I'll let people use it, but for the most part, I'm not into that. I'm into trying to do something good with this thing; I want to come up with something real, something profound, something that you can stick your teeth into.

SP: *Do you believe that you can be commercial and deep artistically at the same time?*

MG: Oh, yes you can. It takes a strong insight into people and personalities, and knowing what the people like and what they want, and not being too far left or too far right, but showing your individuality and personality but not taking it into radicalism. It's quite easy to be commercial and still be creative because you have to understand that the bottom line is that they'll listen to your message if they like your song. And how do you get them to like your song? By putting your message in a vehicle that they're used to, that isn't a copy, but is in the mold or sphere or the range of where music is at this particular time. And it only takes a bit of observing and a bit of going out and watching and listening to the kids. I mean it's not very difficult to stay current, if you like that sort of thing and want to do it.

SP: *Do you listen to much radio for inspiration? How does Marvin Gaye really write a song?*

MG: No, frankly, I don't. I cannot get anything from listening to a radio a lot. I have to get a conglomeration of stuff. I have to listen a little bit to the radio, watch a little television, watch my daughter, watch the kid 'round the block, watch a fight in the street, try and break that up. See a dance, see a chick that looks great, then after I get all this, I get all this stuff in me and feel the beat and the pulse of all this, then I kinda figure that this is where it all is. But it keeps me writing originally, because that way I don't focus in on any one thing or one sound or one overall sound, or anything. Then I can keep my originality intact because I'm not saying, "Hey, this is the sound that will do it." My sound is just sorta everything. This is what it is. I'm stepping a little deeper into an interesting thing with my new album.

SP: *How much do you miss the old Motown days?*

MG: I imagine that if I asked Smokey Robinson or Stevie Wonder or Diana Ross to play on my album they would, just like in the olden days. And I'm still a pretty fair drummer, if it isn't something too complicated; for holding down some simple rhythms, I'm pretty steady. We did that in those days because we were learning and we were eager to learn. I was eager to be with music and be a part of music, and I'd learn anything and do anything. Even though I don't feel we got near the compensation for that, song royalties and everything, it was still a vehicle for us to create. So, one hand washed the other.

SP: *Are you bitter about anything?*

MG: If you're not bitter about money, which I am sometimes . . . but most of the time I'm not, no. I really did a lot of those things very willingly because it was there and I wanted to see if I could do it, see if I could play drums. I could be a drummer, I could be a singer, I could be a horn player, I could be anything, and I'll try it. It was good for us all. Stevie Wonder and myself, we used to hang in the studio and practice and play different things, us and Smokey Robinson, we'd do that for hours. We might come up with a big smash during the day. It was okay because . . . we didn't make a lot of money, but it was okay. We started out with the right spirit, and I think, I know for a fact, that at heart, that Berry Gordy has a great heart. I know that, I can say that. Of course, he's also a businessman, and a good one. Having a great heart and being a businessman can be a lot of trouble, but he manages to do it pretty well. I have my gripes, everybody does, but I guess that's to be expected.

SP: *How do you feel about dancing now, and the fact that disco seems to be the thing? Marvin Gaye was never really much of a dancer, was he?*

MG: Yeah. Dance is very good. People don't dance enough. What people should do is, people should learn when they study their roots, they should incorporate their roots as they take themselves back. Because everybody danced; they all had a certain way that they danced, and they should incorporate their roots into their regular modern-day dance. It's very simple to do, and basically what we do anyway. We haven't had long enough to get away from our roots or our roots reflect our dance a little more ethnically, vividly then perhaps with yourself. It's good for the soul. I think on this world you are put as a people, you have your different feelings which you communicate through the dance, from your soul. And, whatever your soul does, this is how your dance comes out. That's why everyone does different dances, the Indians, and the Irish, and the Scottish, and the Africans, everyone does their own. In Africa, they have their little different dances, tribal things, and what happens is that it's very good for you physically for relieving tension, for letting your emotions out, for expressing sexual desires or feelings, for getting rid of inhibitions. The dance is very necessary in society. I was the type of person who never felt the dance, I always wondered why, what was wrong with my soul that I could never feel the dance. And, I'm still having a lot of trouble feeling the dance. I don't know what I dance, but everybody always says it's really dorky.

I used to go out to parties, and stand around 'cause I was really nervous. A time back, a year or so ago, I began to dance a little on stage. I mean never before would I dance; I'd just come out and pop my fingers and figure that everybody would think I chose to be cool. Which is always a possibility as long as you don't try to dance. Once they've discovered that you're really ridiculous, you've blown it. I really wasn't a great dancer, and I don't consider myself a great dancer now.

SP: *Who are some great dancers?*

MG: I consider Jackie Wilson a great dancer, or James Brown. I really don't know why I can't get off into really getting down and dancing. I'm trying; I'm still working on it. Maybe when I'm older it will even be nicer. If I'm still in show business when I'm 50, and really getting down with whatever the dance would be at that time. It'll probably be something really wild.

SP: *What is disco all about?*

MG: To me there are two types of dance tunes, disco and funk, and "Give It Up," this new song is a funk tune, meaning it's got a chant to it; it's got a round type of overplay, like at the end, it's got two chants going simultaneously, and the bass line is hypnotic. Disco is more monotonous.

SP: *Your career has been very curious—why so?*

MG: I think I have a special talent. In fact, I know I have a special talent. Yes, my career is a very curious one, if one is into that sort of thing and if you know anything about my career. I know it's quite a curious career, it's curious to me and I'm in it.

It takes time to develop; I feel I'm still developing and I don't know what I'm going to go off to, but I feel like I told you earlier—it's going to be something phenomenal.

I know that if I stay with my music, and keep my head on the proper level, I'm going to do some fantastic music. I mean, music that will transcend perhaps music, I hope.

SP: *To many, you are an enigma—first going into being a recluse then surfacing again.*

MG: I'm a little mischievous in my music. If you notice, I like to play. I want everybody, as long as I'm here, to say, "I wonder what Marvin Gaye is going to do." I don't know what I'm going to do. I know what I ain't gonna do, and what I ain't gonna do is come back with something pretty much like what I did or have done. To me, that's a job that's finished and I'm off to new adventures. I can't do four albums a year. I don't think I can, not on me. Maybe I could produce four other acts, but I couldn't do four on me.

SP: *How many people know Marvin Gaye?*

MG: I think very few people know me, 'cause I won't allow it. There's only one or two people in the world who really know me; I've allowed them to look into my mirror. Personally, I can't let a lot of people look inside 'cause I haven't gotten a lot of things together yet . . . I am a very receptive being. I'd say I have my senses geared to receive. It doesn't come through me, but to me from somewhere else. The reason I know it's true is that I'm guided so strangely in my career and my life, that it's almost like I have no control over even my music sometimes. It's like here comes this new song—here it is, let's put on the tape. And I'm still working like mad, and I should just relax and let this force do its stuff. But I can't do that. I have to get involved in ego and stuff and think that I am worth something, and that's probably why I have the problems I have.

SP: *How does the creative process work for you, vibes and all?*

MG: Those vibes will have to work . . . on a different level, and on a top level those vibes will have to come together for the security of all record companies. It's kind of rough out there and together this is the one thing that will save many, many independents. I enjoy working that way. I am basically made up to work that way. I'm a team person. I believe in team sports, team work, and I enjoy that. We got away from that, and what can I say . . .

SP: *How about artists you want to produce?*

MG: Yeah, and I'll let them do their things also. If they have faith in me and want me to totally do my thing, and trust me implicitly, trust that I'm going to take them and carry them someplace else. I can do that. There are levels of control from A to Z that I'll allow, also, until it starts to affect me creatively. When it starts to affect me creatively, I'll probably cut the project off.

SP: *How have you been able to maintain this balance that you've managed to create for yourself?*

MG: Life is a set of scales. You have to balance or you'll tilt and become lop-sided in life. You have to learn to balance things out. I mean if you go out tonight and stay up all night until 7 AM in the morning, you can't go out the next night and do that, the next two days you've got to get some rest. That's balance, and perhaps you offset that, perhaps you save yourself later in years the penalty to pay for that because you've balanced out that hanging out 'til six when your body should be resting. It's ridiculous that we don't do these little common sense things, so then you start to learn about balance. If you know that much, and you're intelligent enough to know that and to balance that out, then I don't think you'll have to worry about that individual because you'll learn how to balance things. It's kind of scientific. There is a formula for living that's very scientific and people should probably get off into it . . . the science of living.

SP: *What do you think about the times we live in?*

MG: I think these are very ridiculous times, and I've been part of the ridiculousness, and I've enjoyed it, knowing that I shouldn't be, knowing that there are more profound things to do, higher sights and goals to work on. And I really don't have any time for this tomfoolery; but I'll have to try harder. I really think it's ridiculous out there watching the permissiveness of the times and the apathy of the times, and the . . .

SP: *Corporatization of the times?*

MG: Well, even that I could put up with if there weren't a lot of crazy other things happening that make life rather unbearable. The times could be good. There are some really decent people in the world; there are also a lot of people who aren't, particularly. But I really think all those who aren't particularly nice, are really crying for help to learn how to be decent. Innately we all know that's what we should strive and reach for. That is the sun, becoming one with God and knowing a little bit about what the Almighty's like; we need a lot of work and a lot of time. I mean that you know that you are so far away from obtaining that kind of control that it's ridiculous. You can't begin to light a match to yourself. It takes a lifetime to gain that peace.

SP: *How does your religious background balance out with the crassness of the world we live in today?*

MG: I put up with it.

SP: *Why do you put up with it?*

MG: I don't know; it just seems it exists. No, it really isn't that difficult. This is the way life is supposed to be, according to those in control. That's what it really is, that's all it is, and those people who are in control are not that many, but they're very powerful, and you simply bend to the power because you don't want the power to be angry and come down on you, because you know the might of the power. So you yield to the power and if your human rights, or if some of your rights are stepped on, you yield to that. It is the power and you are one, and even when you are two, that isn't enough. And it all seems so useless when you think about how it can be changed, and the time it takes, and what it goes through, and how it can be squashed anywhere along the road. How you'll have to get up hundreds of thousands of people to be heard or put any pressure on the power.

SP: *But how does one go about dealing with this?*

MG: If you can't deal with all those things, you might as well forget about it. Either you're a revolutionist or you're not. It's a very nasty word that people are afraid of. Nobody really understands the word. There are a lot of people that, if you mention the word "revolutionist," they think of anarchy and overthrowing the government, all that kind of stuff. But you can be a revolutionary, and when you are that way, you are concerned with human rights, basic human rights, and if you are really a true revolutionary, you will die. You will give up the ultimate, and that is what the power fears. It fears the result of the true revolutionary who will die for the right to say you all are wrong, and I will die because you all are wrong, and I'll show the world the heart I have for them, the deep love that I have for people. I chose not to live under this type of oppression, and I will die 'cause I chose to fight the oppressor. Then the others will say, I like the oppressor because he's powerful and he's all right with me.

SP: *Where does the control factor come in?*

MG: We don't have any control over what they're doing, it's really a lot of money for what we pay, and for what we take. Handcuffs for a parking ticket; it's degrading. It makes you feel less than a man. Why do I have to be handcuffed for a parking violation because I didn't pay you your money? What if your machine made a mistake and my human rights were being violated for no reason? If I was really a man I wouldn't accept it. But, alas, who wants to die? They know that and they understand it. But somebody has to say, "This has to stop!" Like for instance, the power is afraid of a lie detector; they refuse to even say it's accurate because it would put the judge out of business.

SP: *So how do you fight all that stuff? How do you live in a system that you feel is basically against us?*

MG: Well, the system isn't basically against anybody. The system has to have power. I'm probably not an anarchist, but I could live very well in a society where I was the only person I had to answer to, and I'd take my chances. I

don't do well being governed; I never did. I don't think
that I should be governed. I think I could govern very
well; but, I don't think that I should be governed. And
there aren't enough people who feel they shouldn't be
governed. I can govern myself very nicely.

1. Blaxploitation films of the early and mid-1970s also made use of the conflict between blacks and Italians but in a way more favorable to blacks than the "Rocky" films. In these films, most of the gangsters that were flooding the ghetto with drugs and whom the hero usually killed at film's end were Italian. One finds a number of unflattering, at times racist, references to Italian-Americans in the 1960s works of LeRoi Jones (see particularly *Home: Social Essays, Dutchman, The Toilet*, and *The System of Dante's Hell*). As one learns from both *The System of Dante's Hell* and Baraka's autobiography (*The Autobiography of LeRoi Jones/Amiri Baraka*), Baraka grew up in Newark, New Jersey, among Italian ethnics and experienced how racist they could be.

2. The second *Imitation of Life* film, starring Lana Turner and released in 1959, reworks some aspects of the first film, but the struggle between the dark black mother and her white-looking child is the same. In this version, a white actress plays the role of the black woman's daughter. She is humiliatingly and abusively rejected by her white male lover when it is revealed that she is black, much as Natalie Wood's character is in *Kings Go Forth*. It is interesting that the second *Imitation of Life* and the film version of *Porgy and Bess* came out the same year that Lorraine Hansberry's play *A Raisin in the Sun* hit the stage.

3. This film is clearly a reworking of the knights of the Round Table and the quest for the grail. If seen in this light, it is actually interesting but still flawed. After all, Sinatra and his buddies do not get the money in the end.

4. Even though there had been some jazz presentations in temples of high culture before this concert, the Goodman Carnegie Hall performance brought jazz into the concert hall permanently. It was, at this time, very radical and daring to have a jazz performance in such a

place. Moreover, Goodman gave a programmatic history of jazz that was racially integrated, as was his band.

5. Of course, rap music is different in that the performers are trying to adopt the guise of gangsters and degenerates. This was not true in earlier forms of popular dance music, although clearly the performers saw themselves as outsiders or as different.

6. For a sense of what black business was like before Motown as it was described in pre-1960 studies, see *The Negro as a Business Man* by J.H. Harmon, Jr., Arnett G. Lindsay, and Carter G. Woodson (McGrath, 1969) and *The Negro in American Business: The Conflict between Separatism and Integration* by Robert H. Kinzer and Edward Sagarin (Greenberg, 1950).

7. The military was a significant career for black men at the time that Gordy joined. It had been integrated by executive order issued by President Truman in 1948, so blacks now had considerable opportunity for career advancement in the military, particularly as the process of integration was accelerated by the Korean War (1950–53). There were also the benefits of the GI Bill.

8. Creating a kind of symmetry, in 1960, Poitier starred in a Korean War film called *All the Young Men,* where he played the leader of a company of white soldiers who were unsure of his abilities. This is a bit like *No Way Out* (1950), with which Poitier opened the decade.

9. For complementary accounts of the Robinson/Robeson affair, see *The Era: 1947–1957, when the Yankees, the Giants, and the Dodgers Ruled the World* by Roger Kahn (Ticknor and Fields, 1993); *Jackie Robinson: A Biography* by Arnold Rampersad (Knopf, 1997); and *Paul Robeson* by Martin Duberman (Knopf, 1988).

10. Sammy Davis, Jr., gives a vivid account of his breaking the color line at the Copa in his autobiography, *Yes I Can* by Sammy Davis, Jr., and Jane and Burt Boyar (Farrar, Straus and Giroux, 1965).

Selected Bibliography

Benjaminson, Peter. *The Story of Motown.* Groove Press, 1979.

Bjorn, Lars (with Jim Gallert). *Before Motown: A History of Jazz in Detroit, 1920–1960.* University of Michigan Press, 2001.

Davis, Sharon. *Motown: The History.* Guiness Publications, 1988.

Dr. Licks. *Standing in the Shadow of Motown: The Life and Music of Legendary Bassist James Jamerson.* Dr. Licks Publishing, 1989.

Edmonds, Ben. *Marvin Gaye: What's Going On and the Last Days of the Motown Sound.* Mojo Books, 2001.

George, Nelson. *Where Did Our Love Go? The Rise and Fall of the Motown Sound.* St. Martin's Press, 1986.

Gordy, Berry, Sr. *Movin' Up: Pop Gordy Tells His Story.* Harper and Row, 1979.

Gordy, Berry. *To Be Loved: The Music, the Magic, the Memories of Motown.* Warner, 1994.

Jackson, Michael. *Moonwalk.* Doubleday, 1988.

Morse, David. *Motown and the Arrival of Black Music.* Collier Books, 1972.

Posner, Gerald L. *Motown: Money, Power, Sex, and Music.* Random House, 2002.

Reeves, Martha (with Mark Bego). *Dancing in the Street: Confessions of a Motown Diva.* Hyperion, 1994.

Ritz, David. *Divided Soul: The Life of Marvin Gaye.* Da Capo Press, 1991.

Robinson, Smokey (with David Ritz). *Smokey: Inside My Life.* McGraw-Hill, 1989.

Singleton, Raynoma Gordy (with Bryan Brown and Mim Eichler).
Berry, Me, and Motown: The Untold Story. Contemporary
Books, 1990.

Smith, Suzanne E. *Dancing in the Street: Motown and the Cultural
Politics of Detroit.* Harvard University Press, 1999.

Taraborrelli, J. Randy. *Motown: Hot Wax, City Cool, and Solid
Gold.* Doubleday, 1986.

Taraborrelli, J. Randy. *Call Her Miss Ross: The Unauthorized Biography of Diana Ross.* Birch Lane Press, 1989.

Taraborrelli, J. Randy. *Michael Jackson: The Magic and the Madness.*
Carol Publishing Group, 1991.

Turner, Steve. *Trouble Man: The Life and Death of Marvin Gaye.*
Ecco Press, 2000.

Turner, Tony (with Barbara Aria). *All That Glittered: My Life with
the Supremes.* Penguin, 1990.

Turner, Tony (with Barbara Aria). *Deliver Us from Temptation.*
Thunder's Mouth Press, 1992.

Waller, Don. *The Motown Story.* Scribner, 1985.

Whitall, Susan. *Women of Motown: An Oral History,* edited by Dave
Marsh. Avon Books, 1998.

Williams, Otis (with Patricia Romanowski). *Temptations.* Simon and
Schuster, 1989.

Wilson, Mary (and Patricia Romanowski). *Dreamgirl: My Life as a
Supreme.* St. Martin's Press, 1986.

Wilson, Mary (and Patricia Romanowski). *Supreme Faith: Someday
We'll Be Together.* HarperCollins, 1990.

Selected Books on African-American Music

Baraka, Amiri. *Blues People: Negro Music in White America.* William
Morrow, 1983.

Bowman, Bob. *Soulsville U.S.A.: The Story of Stax Records.* Schirmer Books, 1997.

Floyd, Samuel A. *The Power of Black Music: Interpreting Its History from Africa to the United States.* Oxford University Press, 1996.

George, Nelson. *The Death of Rhythm and Blues.* Pantheon Books, 1988.

Gregory, Hugh. *The Real Rhythm and Blues.* London: Blandford Books, 1998.

Guralnick, Peter. *Sweet Soul Music: Rhythm and Blues and the Southern Drama of Freedom.* Harper and Row, 1986.

Murray, Albert. *Stomping the Blues.* Da Capo Press, 1989.

Neal, Mark Anthony. *What the Music Said: Black Popular Music and Black Public Culture.* Routledge, 1998.

Porter, Eric. *What Is This Thing Called Jazz? African American Musicians as Artists, Critics, and Activists.* University of California Press, 2002.

Pruter, Robert. *Chicago Soul.* University of Illinois Press, 1991.

Southern, Eileen J. *The Music of Black Americans: A History,* 3d ed. Norton, 1997.

Ward, Brian. *Just My Soul Responding: Rhythm and Blues, Black Consciousness, and Race Relations.* University of California Press, 1998.

Werner, Craig. *A Change Is Gonna Come: Music, Race, and the Soul of America.* Plume Books, 1999.

Index